About the Author

Moustafa Gadalla was born in Cairo in 1944. He graduated from Cairo University with a Bachelor of Science in civil engineering in 1967. He immigrated to the U.S.A. in 1971 and continued to practice engineering as a Licensed Professional Engineer and Land Surveyor. He is an independent Egyptologist who spent most of his adult life studying, researching scores of books about Egyptology, mythology, religions, the Bible, languages, etc. He often lectures and writes articles about ancient Egypt. He spends a few months of every year in Egypt visiting and studying sites of antiquities.

As an engineer by training and practice, he approaches the issue analytically, logically and writes the findings and conclusions in a rational and easy to understand way.

Visit our website at:
http://members.aol.com/USHorus

Other Books By Author

Historical Deception
The Untold Story of Ancient Egypt
ISBN: 0-9652509-5-4 (pbk.), 352 pages
$19.95 Pub. in 1996 by Bastet Publishing

Pyramid Illusions
A Journey to the Truth
ISBN: 0-9652509-7-0 (pbk.), 192 pages
$11.95 Pub. in 1997 by Bastet Publishing

Dedicated
to
Ancient Egypt
The Eternal Light

Credits

Moustafa Gadalla: for cover design
Sean Sexauer: for typing and computer work
Mark Weber: for interior illustrations
Faith Cross: for interior book design

Tut-Ankh-Amen

The Living Image of the Lord

Moustafa Gadalla

Bastet Publishing, Erie, Pa., U.S.A.

Tut-Ankh-Amen
The Living Image of the Lord

by MOUSTAFA GADALLA

Published by:

Bastet Publishing
Post Office Box 7234
Erie, PA. 16510, U.S.A.

Printed in the United States of America, 1997

Cataloging in Publication Data

Gadalla, Moustafa.
Tut-Ankh-Amen : The Living Image of the Lord / Moustafa Gadalla.

p. cm.
Includes bibliographical references and index.
Preassigned LCCN: 97-92976
ISBN: 0-9652509-9-7 (pbk.)

1. Tutankhamen, King of Egypt. 2. Jesus Christ--Historicity. 3. Egypt--History--To 640 A.D. 4. Egypt--Antiquities. 5. Egypt--Religion. 6. Egypt in the Bible. I. Title.

DT87.5.G34 1997 932'.014
QBI97-40313

Manufactured in the United States of America
Published 1997

Table of Contents

♦♦♦♦♦♦♦♦♦♦♦♦ Epilogue ♦♦♦♦♦♦♦♦♦♦♦♦

Preface

Over the last two thousand years, people have been searching for the historical existence/evidence of Jesus and other major biblical characters (Moses, David, Solomon, ...etc.). All these efforts have been fruitless because most people have accepted the biblical stories as historical events and went out searching for the evidence to support their pre-determined conclusions.

Common sense suggests the exact opposite direction in our search for the historical Jesus and other biblical characters. We should investigate what the historical evidence says about the biblical events and not the other way around.

Most scholars have now accepted the fact that the Bible is a blend of history and fiction, shaped by the political and religious disputes of ancient times. The pivotal dispute in the Bible is the Exodus. As a result of the Exodus, the Bible tarnished the history of ancient Egypt and set in motion the ongoing blood feud in the Middle East.

The topics of this book do not discuss new discoveries, but bring to light historical events, which have been ignored by many Egyptologists because of the risk of contradicting popular religions and especially the true identification of Jesus. It is the intention of this book to identify the historical Christ, not to contend the religious interpretations of his life and teachings that developed subsequently.

☥ King Tut's birth name was Tut-Ankh-Aton, which translated means *The Living Image of the Lord*.

☥ King Tut, like all Egyptian pharaohs, was the spiritual Son of God and was called the Messiah/Christ, meaning the *annointed one,* who is *the King.*

Let us examine the powerful evidence from archaeology, the Dead Sea Scrolls, the Talmud and the Bible itself. Let us discover the history's greatest conspiracy and cover-up to re-create the character of Jesus living in another place and time.

All the evidence points to the identification of Tut-Ankh-Amen as the historical Jesus. This will be, for many people, a troubling statement. The evidence, however, leads us directly to this logical conclusion.

Establishing the historical identity of Jesus should strengthen rather than weaken people's faith in him.

Love and respect for Jesus the man should not change because of his nationality. His message and achievements should be carried on.

Let us open our minds and review the available evidence. For the truth is a composite of different and complementary pieces of a puzzle. Let us put the pieces in the right location, time and order.

Moustafa Gadalla

Standards and Terminology

1- It was a common practice, for the ancient Egyptians, to have several names. It was also the custom to use pet names as well as abbreviated names for longer and more complex names. The name was not a mere label, as per our modern day thinking. Each name had a specific meaning and function.

As such, each person had a composite-type name. The names usually indicated the neter (god) under whom the person concerned was placed e.g. **Re**-mos, **Ptah**-hotep, Tut-Ankh-**Amen**, and so on.

2- As in all Semitic styles of writings, hieroglyphic writing was limited to the consonants of the words, because the meaning of the word was generally contained in the consonants, while the vowels were added only to indicate the grammatical forms. As such, vowel sounds were not included in the written language.

Since we do not know the exact sounds of their words, and to simplify matters, scholars agreed to a certain way of pronunciation. Therefore, the vowels you see in translated Egyptian texts are an approximation, and by no means is it the true sound.

As a result, you may find a variety in writing the same thing such as Aten/Aton, Amen/Amon/Amun, Mery/Mary/Merry. The *A* at the beginning of the word is not considered a vowel by the ancients, but rather a consonant.

Likewise, the pronunciation and interpretation of the ancient vowel-less Hebrew texts were accomplished by a body of Jewish scholars, between the seventh and tenth centuries A.D.

3- We have gotten accustomed to repeating wrongly interpreted words and names, from the ancient Egyptian texts. Such as:

a- The ancient Egyptian word *neter*, and its feminine form *netert*, have been wrongly, and possibly intentionally, translated to *god* and *goddess*, by almost all scholars. There is no equivalent word in meaning, to the word *neter*, in the English language. Honest translators should use the native word, if they cannot find its equivalent in their language.
Neteroo (plural of neter/netert) are the divine principles and functions that operate the universe. They are all aspects and functions of the One Supreme God.
The words *god* and *goddess* leave the impression that ancient Egyptians had a multitude of *gods*, which is absolutely untrue.

b- The names *Twtankhamen* and *Twthomosis* have been written by many scholars as *Tutankamen* and *Tuthomosis*. The second letter in their names is the consonant *w*, and not the vowel *u*.
For simplicity sake (even though incorrect) this book will show the names as Tut-Ankh-Amen and Tuthomosis.

4- Throughout this book, fonting of quotations varies depending on the source of quotation. There are generally three types of fonting, ***one for the Bible and Talmud,*** **a second for ancient Egyptian records**, and *a third for Egyptologists and other scholars.*

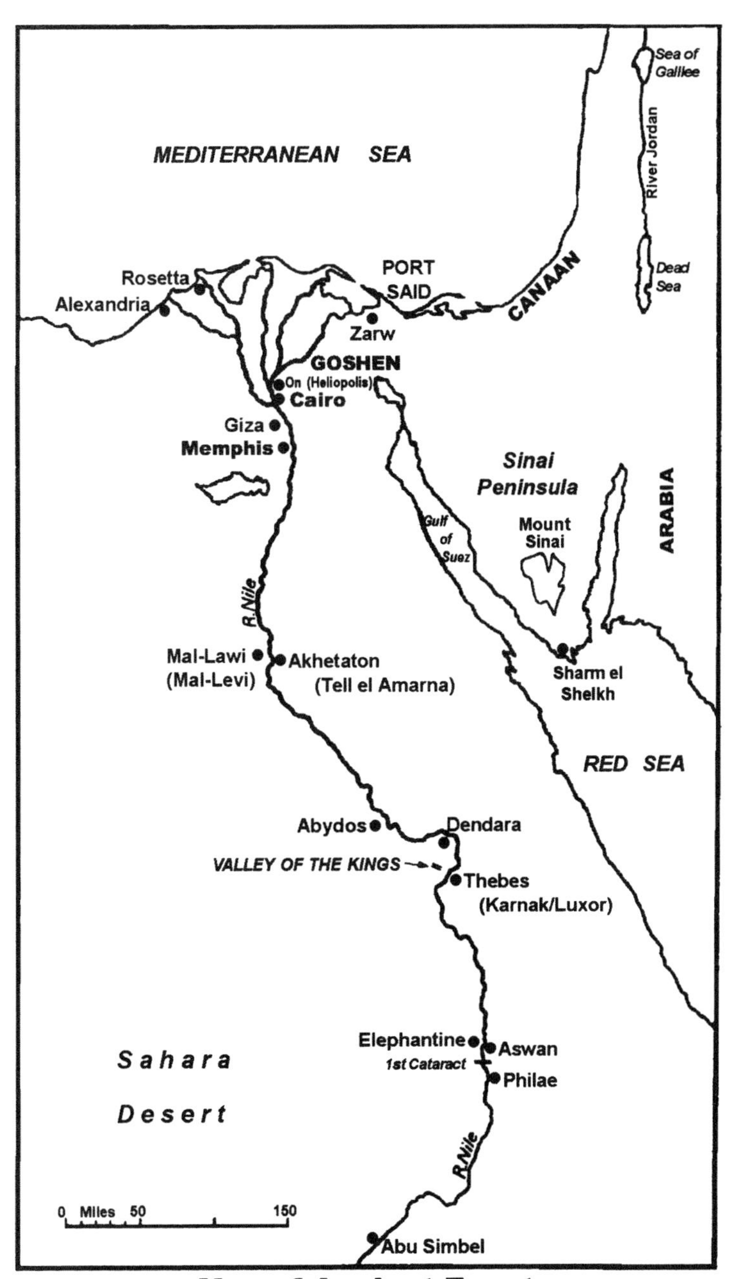

Map of Ancient Egypt

Prologue

1

Jesus and History

The Common Story (The Gospels)

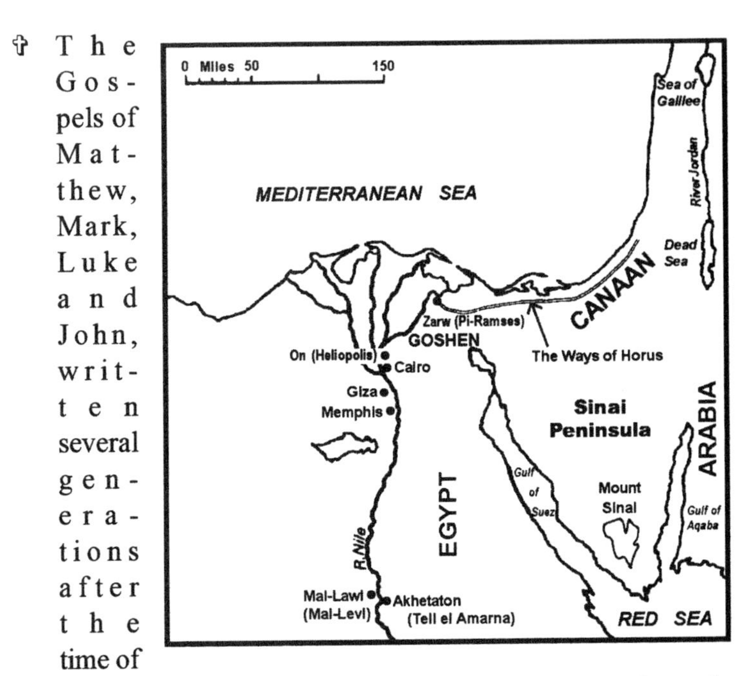

✞ The Gospels of Matthew, Mark, Luke and John, written several generations after the time of the events they describe, state that Jesus was born in Judaea (which lies between the Mediterranean and the Jordan - Dead Sea - Arab depression) during the time of Herod the Great (37-4 B.C.), and that his condemnation to death, suffering and crucifixion occurred when Judaea had become a Roman province with Pontius Pilate as its procurator (26-36 A.D.).

- ✝ Despite the existence of many Gospels of Christ in the early history of the Church, Council of Trent in 1546 only accepted the four included in the New Testament - those of Matthew, Mark, Luke and John.

- ✝ Mark, who is named in the New Testament's Book of Acts and in four Epistles as a companion of Peter and Paul, is presumed to have been the author of the earliest of the four canonical Gospels. The other three (Matthew, Luke and John) relied on the writings attributed to Mark, plus other sources, for their writings.

- ✝ Mark was not an eyewitness to the events that he described in the Bible. Neither were Matthew, Luke or John, who followed him later.
  Mark may have had the benefit of second-hand information from Peter and third-hand from Paul. The Gospel of Mark, however, includes information which is not mentioned in the writings of Peter and Paul!

☞ Where did Mark get this information from? Mark must have used the following available sources, to compile the stories, to place the life of Jesus in Galilee at this period of history:

1- Israelite traditions
2- The Old Testament
3- The practices of the Jewish Sect of Essenes (the owners of the Dead Sea Scrolls)
4- The life and death of John the Baptist
5- The political upheavals of the first century A.D.

☞ **The "common" story, by the Gospels, of the life and death of Jesus has <u>no</u> corroborative evidence to support it. Only its continuous repetition to us has made it appear as an established fact.**

The Evidence Against the Gospel Accounts

1- The Dead Sea Scrolls

✡ The world was excited in 1947 and the following years, when the Dead Sea Scrolls were discovered. The Dead Sea Scrolls were found in a series of caves at Qumran, west of the north end of the Dead Sea. They consist of the remains of the Library of a Jewish sect called the Essenes and are dated between 200 B.C. and 50 A.D.

✞ The Essenes is a secret Jewish sect which separated from the Jewish community at large. They regard the beliefs and teachings of the Jerusalem priesthood to be untrue.

✞ The Scrolls include biblical and sectarian texts, Jewish literature and other documents. The Scrolls don't include information about the biblical Jesus but they provide information of a Christ and a Christian church that predates the supposed start of the Christian era by several centuries.

✞ About 80% of these scrolls remain unpublished and the results of their findings are being kept secret from the world. The contents of the few released scrolls, which pre-date the Gospels, provide the following:

- An account of the Annunciation which reads almost exactly like Luke (1:28-35).

- A clear statement that the Essenes believed that the Messiah had already lived and was later killed by the Wicked Priest (who is identified in the Talmud as Pinhas/Phinehas, the priest who killed the biblical Jesus).

- The Essenes, in 200 B.C., were awaiting the Messiah's Second Coming, not the first.

✞ The very name of the Essenes indicate that they were followers of Jesus. Essenes means *Followers of Essa.* Essa is the Arabic name for Jesus. Essa is the only name of Jesus to be mentioned in the Koran and was the name used by the early Egyptian Christians in the Coptic Egyptian language, in the first century A.D.

✞ The Dead Sea Scrolls, which date to 200 B.C., contain some accounts of the Gospel accounts of the birth, life and death of Jesus. In short, the Essenes and their scrolls are the best proof yet that Jesus lived several centuries earlier than the common belief.

2- Moses and Jesus of the Same Era

Contrary to common beliefs, there are several accounts in the New Testament, the Old Testament and the Talmud, that show that the biblical Jesus and Moses were of the same era.

a- In the New Testament

✞ The Bible itself confirms that Jesus lived fourteen centuries earlier than had been thought. Note the event described in the Gospels of Matthew, Mark and Luke, about the meeting of Jesus and Moses, at the time of what is known as his Transfiguration:

"And after six days Jesus taketh with him Peter, and James, and John, and leadeth them up into a high mountain apart by themselves: and he was transfigured before them. And his rai-

ment became shining, exceeding white as snow; so as no fuller on earth can white them. And they appeared unto them Elias (Elijah) with Moses: and they were talking with Jesus. And Peter answered and said to Jesus, Master, it is good for us to be here: and let us make three tabernacles; one for thee, and one for Moses, and one for Elias ..." (Mark, 9:2-5)

The biblical text is a straight forward factual description of an event. It is irrational to view the factual nature of this text as simply some kind of a *spiritual experience* and that it never actually happened!!

Some people want to consider this meeting event a *spiritual experience* yet they insist that the virgin birth and the Resurrection of Christ were actual historical events!!

✞ John confirms that Jesus lived fourteen centuries earlier than his prescribed time. John quotes Jesus as telling the Jews of Jerusalem: ***'For had ye believed Moses, ye would have believed me: for he wrote of me'*** (John, 5:46). The biblical verse clearly states that Moses wrote of Jesus.

John also refers to Philip, one of the disciples, regarding the same fact: ***'Philip findeth Nathanael, and saith unto him, We have found him, of whom Moses in the law, and the prophets, did write, Jesus of Nazareth, the son of Joseph'*** (John, 1:45). According to John, Moses wrote (not as a prophesy) about Jesus in the Pentateuch, the first five books of the Old Testament.

- John, after using a reference to Isaiah to report some of the activities of Jesus, goes on to say: *'Isaiah said this because he saw his glory, and spoke of him'* (John, 12:41). John is stating that Isaiah saw the *glory* of Jesus. However, Jesus is said to have achieved *glory* only after his death and Resurrection: *'... God, that raised him up from the dead and gave him glory ...'* (I Peter, 1:21), and also: *'... the sufferings of Christ and the glory that should follow'* (I Peter, 1:11). To summarize, John acknowledged that Christ lived and died before the time of Isaiah's writings.

- Paul, in his first Epistle to the Corinthians, makes clear that Jesus was present with the Israelites in Sinai at the time of the Exodus: *'Moreover, brethren, I would not that ye should be ignorant, how that all our fathers were under the cloud, and all passed through the sea; And were all baptized unto Moses in the cloud and in the sea; And did all eat the same spiritual meat; And did all drink the same spiritual drink: for they drank of the spiritual Rock that followed them: and that Rock was Christ'* (I Corinthians, 10:1-4).

  Paul is stating here that the Rock really was Christ, i.e. the Messiah was present in some form with the Israelites during the Exodus.

- Further confirmation of Jesus' presence with the Israelites in the Sinai wilderness is also stated in Paul's Epistle to the Hebrews where, after referring to the disobedient Israelites *who left Egypt under Moses*, he says: *'For unto us was the gospel preached, as well as unto them: but the word preached did not profit them, not being mixed with faith in them that heard it'* (Hebrews, 4:2).

Paul is stating that the Gospel which was preached in the first century A.D. had been preached before.

b- Jesus' Time in the Old Testament

The Old Testament provides more evidence against the prescribed time of Jesus during the Roman era.

✡ The Gospels define the role given to Jesus as that of a Redeemer, who is to suffer and be sacrificed like a lamb in order to wipe out the sins of his transgressing people. However, the prophetic Old Testament writings of Isaiah (who lived during the second half of the eighth century B.C.), described the same exact character.

✡ Isaiah was the first Israelite prophet to present the Christ as the divinely appointed Savior. The account of the Servant in the Songs of Isaiah (II) also presents, for the first time in the Old Testament, the idea of spiritual salvation and a second life.

✡ The fact that the Old Testament has no Resurrection reference until Isaiah (II), writing in the sixth century B.C., makes it clear that he relied on another, non-biblical, tradition for his account of the risen Christ.

✞ The idea of Christ as the suffering Servant, the Savior of the world and the Redeemer, proves that he had already lived his life and died, i.e. existed before the time of Isaiah (eighth century B.C.).

c- Jesus' Time in the Talmud

✡ The Talmudic rabbis do not relate Jesus to the time of Herod or Pontius Pilate. They do, however, state that a priest named Pinhas killed him. The Talmud is quite specific: '*Pinhas .. killed him* [Jesus]' (b. Sanh., 106b). Pinhas (Phinehas in the Old Testament) was the priest, the son of Eleazar, the son of Aaron, who is identified in the Book of Numbers as a comtemporary of Moses. Read more about Pinhas in the chapters, *Death in the Wilderness* and *The Tyrant Father.*

✡ The Talmudic references to Pinhas/Phinehas and Jesus were ignored because they show Jesus living at the same time as Moses did.

3- Why Was Jesus Not Mentioned by Historians

☞ One wonders, if Jesus lived, suffered and died during the period of Roman rule in Palestine, why did not his name appear in the writings of three distinguished contemporary authors of that time — Philo Judaeus, Justus of Tiberias and Flavius Josephus?!

☞ No reference to Jesus was made in the thirty-eight works left behind by Philo Judaeus, who was born c. 15 B.C. and died about twenty years after the supposed date of the Crucifixion. Philo's brother was the head of the Jewish community living in Alexandria. His son was married to a granddaughter of King Herod.

☞ How can we expect a man like Philo Judaeus, with all his family connections, not to mention Jesus in all his voluminous writings, if Jesus ever existed?!

☞ Flavious Josephus was a Palestinian Jew of a priestly family, born in 37 A.D., who wrote *Antiquities of the Jews*, a long historical work of twenty books.
Moreover, Josephus was given command in Galilee at the time of the Jewish revolt against the Romans in 66 A. D. Flavius Josephus mentioned John the Baptist's life and execution in his books. Josephus never mentioned that John was preparing the way for Jesus or that Jesus existed at all.

☞ The usual response to the historical absence of the Biblical Jesus is that he was an ordinary man and not an important figure to warrant any attention or place in history. The Bible itself provides the contrary evidence to such an incorrect response.

A. Herod, the King of Judea, as per the following biblical verses, knew of Jesus:

1- When Jesus was born ***"..., wise men from the East came to Jerusalem, saying, "Where is he who has been born King of the Jews?..."*** (Matthew, 2:1-2)

2- King Herod was told of a prophecy that the Christ was to be born in Bethlehem, ***"... for from you [Bethlehem] shall come a ruler who will govern my people Israel."*** (Matthew, 2:6)

3- Upon hearing the above prophecy, Herod was

distressed by the news of his birth and therefore Joseph was ordered by the angel of the Lord, *"Rise, take the child and his mother, and flee to Egypt, and remain there till I tell you; for Herod is about to search for the child, to destroy him."* (Matthew, 2:13)

4- Herod was so distressed that he *"sent and killed all the male children in Bethlehem and in all that region who were two years old and under."* (Matthew, 2:16)

5- After Jesus was sentenced to death by the Jewish heirachy, they handed him over to Pilate who *"... when he learned that he belonged to Herod's jurisdiction, he sent him over to Herod, who was himself in Jerusalem at the time."* (Luke, 23:7)

Pilate later told the chief priests, *"I did not find this man guilty of any of your charges against him; neither did Herod, for he sent him back to us."* (Luke, 23:14-16)

B. The Bible tells us that Jesus was a very important figure:

1- Wisemen from different nations came to offer homage to him, as per (Matthew, 2:1-2)

2- He was **born to be King**, as per (Matthew, 2:2)

3- He was born to be a **ruler**, *"... For from you*

shall come a ruler ..." (Matthew, 2:6)

4- He was born to **govern**, *"... who will govern my people Israel"* (Matthew, 2:6)

5- He ruled as a King as per the overwhelming evidence in the chapter, *Jesus, the King.*

C. Jesus was very visible, attracting crowds from all over the region, and causing a lot of commotion, as per the following biblical verses:

1- *"And he went about all Galilee teaching in their synagogue, and preaching the gospel ... so his fame spread throughout all Syria, and they brought him all the sick ... And great crowds followed him from Galilee and ... and from beyond the Jordan."* (Matthew, 4:23-25)

2- *"And those who ate were about five thousand men, besides women and children."* (Matthew, 14:21)

3- *"... a great multitude from Galilee followed; also from Judea and Jerusalem and Id-u-Me'a and from beyond the Jordan and from about Tyre and Si'don a great multitude, hearing all that he did, came to him."* (Mark, 3:7-8)

4- Here is a crowd of more than 9,000 people, *"When I broke the five loaves for the five thousand ... And the seven for the four thousand ..."* (Mark, 8:19-20)

Conclusions

☞ There is not a shred of contemporary evidence to support the New Testament story of the birth, life or death of Jesus.

☞ However, there is an expanse of evidence proving that Jesus had lived many centuries earlier.

☞ The New Testament, the Old Testament and the Talmud place Jesus and Moses in the same era.

The rational way to find the biblical Jesus in history is by examining the historical records. We should examine the records of ancient Egypt.

✞ *"... Out of Egypt have I called my son."* (Matthew, 2:15)

✡ *"Jesus the Nazarene who practiced magic in Egypt."* (b. Sanh., 107b)

2

The Egyptian Connection

Moses and Egypt

In the last chapter, we presented evidence from the New Testament, the Old Testament and the Talmud, proving that Jesus and Moses were of the same era.

The Bible tells us the story of Moses' birth and life in Egypt. The Bible, which is notorious in stating names of persons, sites, and water wells which in many cases have no impact on the story whatsoever, never named a pharaoh or his residence, when an event occurred. There were several pharaohs in Moses' story. The Bible would say, *"The Pharaoh who knew not Joseph"*, or *"Pharaoh of Oppression"*. Wouldn't it have been easier and more logical to use the name of these pharaohs? Why did they leave all their names out? They must have been left out intentionally. But why?

The Exodus at the Root of the Cover-Up

Ancient Egypt and the Israelites had generally a good relationship until Moses and his mother arrived on the scene. (Read the details in the chapter, *The Tyrant Father*.) Their actions resulted in the Exodus, which was a bitter divorce between the Egyptians and the Israelites. Just like any bitter divorce, there were charges and counter charges. The two sides typically ignored each other, but it is the generations which followed (like the children in a divorce case) who paid and will continue to pay the price.

As a result of this bitter divorce, ancient Egypt became the permanent casualty of the *"chosen people"*. The Jewish scribes reflected the political and religious disputes of those ancient times by mixing history and fiction in their writing of the Bible. They changed names and chronology of events to complete their cover-up scheme. As a result, scholars could not, cannot and will not be able to provide a single piece of evidence to confirm the biblical accounts of Jesus, Moses, Solomon, David, ... and others.

The Findings

Based on all available information from the ancient Egyptian historical records, the Bible, the Talmud and the Dead Sea Scrolls, we shall prove that:

Jesus	=	Pharaoh Tut Ankh Amen
Moses	=	Pharaoh Akhenaton
King David	=	Pharaoh Tuthomosis III
King Solomon	=	Pharaoh Amenhotep III

Many reject the notion that such virtuous men could be pharaohs, because of the biblically distorted image of the pharaoh as a harsh tyrant. This is absolutely not true. The Pharaoh was very much like a popular Catholic Pope. His function was fundamentally religious. He was a priest-king.

The comparison between the biblical and the historical characters, in the following chapters, will make the various evidence, individually and collectively, so overwhelming that you will doubt yourself. Please have an open mind.

Son of God/Man

3

His Names

The biblical Jesus and Tut-Ankh-Amen share many similarities, including their variety of names. Below, is a sampling.

1- The Living Image of the Lord

Tut-Ankh-Amen shares this very important name with the biblical Jesus.
Tut's birth name was Tut-Ankh-**Aton**. Tut-Ankh means *the Living Image*. *Aton* signifies the Egyptian neter (god/Lord) who has no image. The Lord of the Jews, who likewise has no image, is called *Adon*. The Egyptian *Aton* is equivalent to the Hebrew *Adon* (the Egyptian *t* becomes *d* in Hebrew). Adonai in Hebrew means *my Lord*. The last two letters *ai* of the word is a Hebrew pronoun meaning *my* or *mine* and signifies possession.
As such, Tut's birth name therefore means *the living image of the Lord*.

2- Messiah/Christ

The English word *Christ* comes from the Greek *Kristos*, which is the equivalent of the Hebrew and Aramaic *Mashih*. The English word *Messiah* originated also from the Hebrew and Aramic *Mashih*, which in its form as a verb *MeSHeH*, means *to anoint*. This word is of Egyptian origin, where *MeSSeH* signified the ritual of anointing ancient Egyptian Kings (including Tut-Ankh-Amen) with the fat of crocodiles, as was the tradition with all kings in ancient Egypt since ca. 2700 B.C.

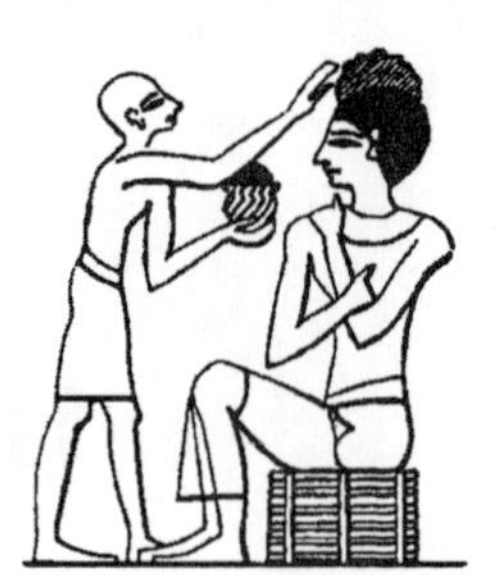

As the letter *s* in Egyptian is equivalent to *sh* in Hebrew and Aramaic, it becomes evident that the biblical word *Messiah* originated from *MeSHeH*, the ancient Egyptian word signifying the ritual of anointing Egyptian Kings. Thus *the Christ/Messiah* means *the anointed one,* who is *the king.*
As such Tut-Ankh-Amen was also Christ, the Messiah.

3- Essa

Essa is the Arabic name of Jesus and the only one used in the Koran. Essa was also the name used for Jesus by the early Egyptian Christians in the Coptic Egyptian language in the first century A.D.

The first followers of Essa (Jesus) were called the Essenes (the owners of the found Dead Sea Scrolls). Philo Judaeus, who wrote the earliest account of this Jewish sect around 30 A.D., called them Essaeans from the Greek *Essaios* but stated that the word was of non-Greek origin. It was recognized that the word *Essene* must have had a Semitic origin, which is *Essa*. *Essaioi* would therefore mean *a follower of Essa.*

☞ **The meanings of Essa and the Essenes were intentionally concealed because the Essenes, as the followers of Essa (Jesus) existed before the time allotted to him during the Romans' time.**

4- Jesus/Joshua

☥ The names *Joshua* (*Ye-ho-shua* in Hebrew) and *Jesus* (*Ye-shua* in its short form), have the same meaning, which is: *Yahweh (the Lord) is salvation.* The Greek text of the Bible reports both names as *Jesus*. The King James Bible and many of the early Church Fathers of the second and third centuries A.D. refer to *Joshua* and *Jesus* as one and the same person.

☥ Ancient Egyptians also believed that *Osiris was salvation.* Osiris came to earth for the benefit of mankind. Osiris manifests the divine in mortal form. Read more about these similarities in the chapter, *Resurrection and Easter.*

5- Ben Pandira (Son of God)

✡ In some Talmudic passages, Jesus is named *Ben Pandira* (the son of Pandira). Since the Jews do not agree that Jesus was the Son of God, they suggested that Pandira was a lover, not the husband, of Mary.

☥ Pandira is a corrupt Hebrew form of an ancient Egyptian royal term. The Hebrew **Pa-ndi-ra**, in its original form, is **Pa-ntr-ra** (pronounced **Pa-neter-ra**). *Ben* means *son.* Ben Pandira, as such, means *Son of God* [Son of the neter (god) Ra]. All Egyptian kings, since ca. 3000 B.C. had the title, **Son of Ra**.

Ra

☞ Thus, *Ben Pandira* (Son of Ra) identifies Jesus as an Egyptian king. The title *son of Ra* is engraved on Tut-Ankh-Amen's stele, which was found in the Karnak Temple in 1905.

6- Immanuel

✡ Three references to Immanuel are made in the Book of Isaiah, such as in 7:14: ***"Therefore the Lord himself shall give you a sign; Behold, a virgin shall conceive, and bear a son, and shall call his name Immanuel".***

Many scholars have noticed that the words used by Isaiah make it clear that the birth had already occured at the time of his writing, i.e. the Messiah had already been born and died, before Isaiah's writing. As such, the story of the biblical Jesus occurred several centuries before the Roman era.

✞ The evangelist, Matthew, regarded Immanuel as another name for Jesus: ***"... they shall call his name Immanuel, which being interpreted is 'God with us'".*** (1:23)

Immanuel could be interpreted in two ways, by dividing the word into its basic elements:

1- Imma-nu (with us) and El (Elohim, God) i.e. *God with us.*
2- Imman-u (his Amun) and El (is God) i.e. *His Amun is God.*

The Hebrew *ayain*, the first letter of Immanuel, is equivalent to the Egyptian *aleph*, which is the first letter of Amun. As discussed in the *Standards and Terminology*, writing the name as Amen/Amon/Amun means the same name. The first interpretation of Immanuel was intentionally highlighted in order to hide the fact that it is the second interpretation which was intended, i.e. His **Amen is God**. This latter interpretation is echoed in King Tut's changing his name from Tut-Ankh-**Aton** to Tut-Ankh-**Amen** four years after he became the King. His new name signified his allegiance to Amen/Amun. Read more about it in the chapter, *The Divided Kingdom.*

4

His Birth

Tut-Ankh-Amen

• Tut-Ankh-Amen was born in the city of Amarna, the capital city of his father, Akhenaton.

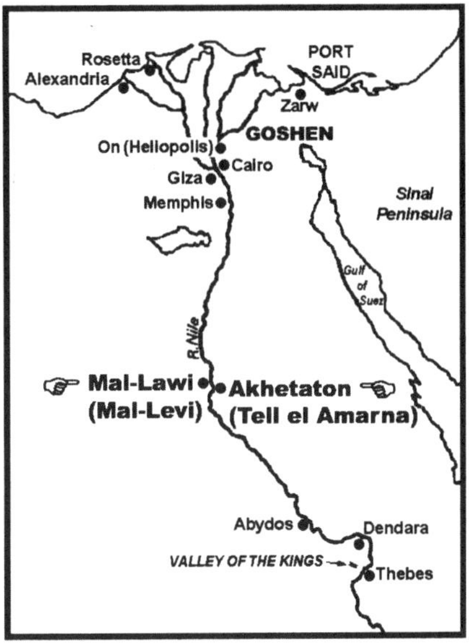

• Amarna was named after Amran (or Imran), which is the name of Akhenaton's god (father) and which is also the name given in the Bible for Moses' father.

• Across the Nile from Tell-el Amarna, there is the city of Mal-lawi (Mal-Levi), which means literally *The City of the Levites*. The Levites, according to the Bible, held priestly positions with Moses, when actually they held the very same positions with Akhenaton (Tut's father).

• The idea of the birth of the Messiah without sexual intercourse originated in ancient Egypt. Isis is said to have conceived her son Horus after her husband's (Osiris) death. The cosmic force responsible for her impregnation was

MeSSeh, the crocodile star, as per Spell 148 of the Coffin Texts: "***The crocodile star (MeSSeH) strikes ... Isis wakes pregnant with the seed of Osiris.***"

• The holy (virgin) birth of the Egyptian king is a recurring theme in temples and writings throughout ancient Egypt. In ancient Egypt, divine birth was looked upon as an aspect of royal birth. Although the child was regarded spiritually as the son of the diety, this did not exclude the human father or the sexual relationship between the parents. In symbolic terms, the Egyptian King was considered to be the ***Son of God***.

The Biblical Jesus

✞ The Gospels' claim, that Jesus was born in Bethlehem, during the Roman Era, has never been proven by any shred of historical evidence.

✞ The birth of Jesus is not mentioned in New Testament writings of the first century A.D.; only the later Gospel writers refer to it. Two of the four Gospels refer to his birth, yet they differ in their details.

✞ By the year 200 A.D., the Church issued the Creed that Jesus Christ was *"conceived by the Holy Ghost"* and *"born of the Virgin Mary"*.

✞ The virgin concept evolved further, when the Council of Trullo in 692 A.D. declared that Mary, the mother of Jesus was *ever-virgin*. This declaration contradicts the following verses of the Bible, stating that Jesus had brothers and sisters:

1- That the biblical Joseph, the supposed husband of Mary, *"...knew her not until she had borne a son."*

(Matthew, 1:25)

2- *"While he was still speaking to the people, behold, his mother and his brothers stood outside, asking to speak to him."* (Matthew, 12:46)

3- *"And are not his brothers James and Joseph and Simon and Judas? And are not all his sisters with us? ..."* (Matthew, 13:56)

4- *"And his mother and his brothers came ..."* (Mark, 3:31)

5- *"... the son of Mary and brother of James and Joses and Judas and Simon, and are not his sisters here with us?"* (Mark, 6:3)

6- *"Then his mother and his brothers came to him ..."* (Luke, 8:19)

7- *"After this he went down to Ca-per'na-um, with his mother and his brothers and his disciples ..."* (John, 2:12)

✞ The virgin idea reached its peak, in the writings of St. Thomas Aquinas, in the thirteenth century. The church endorsed his writing that:

> *"Because she conceived Christ without the defilement of sin, and without the stain of sexual mingling, therefore did she bring him forth without pain, without violation of her virginal integrity, without detriment to the purity of her maidenhood."*

✞ The Virgin Birth, as such, became a historical (not spiritual) fact by the Church.

☞ The released portion of the Dead Sea Scrolls did not mention a virgin mother. The concept of the virgin mother was an afterthought by the later Gospel writers.

The Three Wise Men

The story found in Matthew, about the three wise men who came from foreign countries to offer tribute and presents to the newborn king, is of Egyptian origin. During the time of the Empire such visits and gifts were common practice.

A box was found, in the Valley of the Kings, which contained several pieces of gold leaf, bearing the names of Tut-Ankh-Amen and his uncle Aye. One of these pieces of gold leaf has the two royal cartouches of Aye on one side, faced on the other side by three foreigners whose arms are raised in a position of reverence towards the king's names.

- The first man looks like a typical Syrian from the Mediterranean coast.
- The features of the second man indicate his Sudanese origin.
- The third man represents the white-skinned races of the North, such as Libyans and inhabitants of the Mediterranean islands.

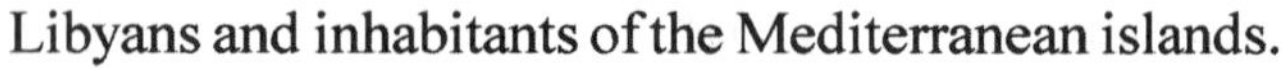

Here, then, is a representation of the three biblical races, Shem, Ham and Japhet. This, therefore, is the original idea of the three wise men, who represented the different people of the ancient known world.

☞ The evidence of the three wise men can only be found in Egypt.

5

His Father

Tut-Ankh-Amen

His father was Akhenaton, as per the evidence presented in answering the following questions:

1- Was Tut-Ankh-Amen the son or brother of Akhenaton?

• As will be detailed later in the chapter *The Tyrant Father*, both Akhenaton and his father Amenhotep III had a co-regency, for twelve years, before Akhenaton ruled alone. According to a shirt found in Tut-Ankh-Amen's tomb, he was born during Akhenaton's Year 7 at Amarna. The shirt evidence provides two conclusions:

A- Since the date on the shirt refers to Akhenaton, therefore and in accordance with the ancient Egyptian practices, Akhenaton was his father.

B- Akhenaton's Year 7 would make Tut-Ankh-Amen ten years of age when he came to the throne and nineteen when he died. These dates are confirmed by anatomical examination of his body, as well as by dated objects found in Tut's tomb.

2- Was Akhenaton's mother, Queen Tiye, the mother or grandmother of Tut-Ankh-Amen?

Tiye

• As stated earlier, Tut-Ankh-Amen was born in Year 7 of his father Akhenaton. During the co-regency of Amenhotep III and Akhenaton, Year 7 of Akhenaton corresponds to Year 33 of Amenhotep III. At such a time, Queen Tiye was about forty-one years old. Two years earlier she had given birth to a daughter, Baketaton.

So, hypothetically Queen Tiye could have been able to give birth to a son, at age forty-one. However, the evidence found in her steward Huya's tomb, indicate that Tiye's first visit to Amarna was during or after Akhenaton's Year 10, i.e. three years after Tut-Ankh-Amen's birth.
The above mentioned shirt indicates a birth in Akhenaton's Year 7 and at Amarna, i.e. when and where Tiye was not present.

Therefore the logical conclusion is that Akhenaton was the father of Tut-Ankh-Amen, and Queen Tiye was the grandmother.

Akhenaton

The Biblical Jesus

✝ Only two of the four Gospels tell us that Joseph the carpenter was Jesus' *shadow* father. The Bible tells us that this Joseph was a descendent of King David.
Notwithstanding all these clear statements, the Bible insists that Jesus, who is not the biological son of this Joseph, was the descendent of King David!

✝ This Joseph disappears from the scene before the supposed ministry of Christ. Nothing is said about his fate!

6

His Mother

Tut-Ankh-Amen

• Since Akhenaton fathered Tut-Ankh-Amen (as proven earlier), his wife, Nefertiti, must have been the mother of Tut-Ankh-Amen.

• Before the birth of Tut-Ankh-Amen, Nefertiti had three daughters, and another three afterwards. From the archaeological findings at Amarna's northern palace, it can be concluded that Nefertiti remained there with her son, Tut-Ankh-Amen, before and after he came to the throne. This also ratifies the maternal relationship.

• Nefertiti's image was used in place of that of Isis, the Egyptian Virgin Mother, on Amarna funerary objects, such as on the sarcophagus of Akhenaton.

☥ There are statues in Rome, originally made to represent Isis and her son Horus, which were used by the Church to represent Mary and her son.

• The name, *Nefertiti*, means ***the beautiful one has come.***

The Biblical Jesus

- The Bible tells us in several locations that Mary, the mother of Jesus, had other children besides Jesus. Read the seven supporting biblical verses under the chapter, *His Birth.*

- The biblical name of Jesus' mother is Mary. The name ***Mary*** is given to many women in the Bible. The two closest women to Jesus were called **Mary**, his mother and **Mary** Magdalene.

- The origin of the name ***Mary*** lies in ancient Egypt, where the written word was **Mr** (the vowels *a* and *y* were added by modern scholars to help pronounce the ancient languages), means *the beloved.*
  The name **Mary/Mery** is one of the most repeated words in ancient Egyptian texts. It was used as an adjective (epithet) before names of people, neteroo (gods), ...etc. This epithet was also applied to many of the Egyptian royal family including his mother, Nefertiti, and his wife, Ankhsenpa-aton.

- The Mother Mary has been described, in the Talmud, as ***"the descendant of princes and rulers"*** (b. Sanh. 106a). This description can only fit Nefertiti, the biblical Madonna.

  The Talmud's description is a direct contradiction to the impression given by the Gospels of Mary's humble roots.

- It was the 6th century B.C. statue of Isis and her son, now in the Turin Museum, which inspired the 15th century painter Masaccio, in his presentation of The Virgin and Child.

7

His Wife

Ankhsenpa-Aton and Tut

- Ankhsenpa-Aton was, as evident from her name, a worshiper of Aton (Adonai in Hebrew).

- As stated on page 44, she was called Mary/Mery which is an Egyptian epithet meaning *beloved.*

- She became the heir to the throne (the line of royal descent was through the eldest daughter - whoever married her became the pharaoh) because:

  - Akhenaton and Nefertiti's eldest daughter married Semenkhkare (Akhenaton's brother and succeeding Pharaoh), who died shortly before the coronation of Tut-Ankh-Amen.

  - Their second daughter had also died.

  - The third daughter Ankhsenpa-aton, in the order of events, became the heiress. Tut-Ankh-Amen married her, and in so doing, he ascended to the throne.

- The couple are shown together in several scenes, always in a relaxed, romantic mode. One can sense her love for Tut-Ankh-Amen, similar to Mary Magdalene's love for the biblical Jesus.

- Alabaster ointment jars were found in the Tut-Ankh-Amen tomb. On the back of his throne, his wife is shown anointing him with perfume exactly as the evangelists described Mary Magdalene anointing the biblical Jesus.

As his wife and queen, she was the only person who could attend his funerary rites, witness the priests announce his Resurrection, and inform his disciples of the news. She is shown doing all that in Tut-Ankh-Amen's tomb.

Mary with Tut, depicted in his tomb, just before Tut ascended to his father

Mary Magdalene and the Biblical Jesus

Mary, a name given to most women in the Bible, meant *beloved* in ancient Egypt, and it was an epithet used before the person's real name. The term *Magdalene* has been explained as belonging to or from the city of Magdala, an unidentified location on the western shore of the Sea of Galilee. The Hebrew word *migdol* means *a tower*. A city named Migdol was located on Horus Road, leading from Egypt to Gaza. Ezekiel 29:10 mentions it: *"... the tower (migdol) of Syene (in the Eastern Delta) even unto the border of Ethiopia".*

This Mary is described in the Bible, as a person who is emotionally related to Jesus.

"there came a woman having an alabaster box of ointment of spikenard very precious; and she brake the box, and poured it on his head" (Mark, 14:3).

"And [she] stood at his feet behind him weeping, and began to wash his feet with tears, and did wipe them with the hairs of her head, and kissed his feet, and anointed them with the ointment" (Luke, 7:38).

As a result of this close relationship, "Mary Magdalene" became one of those who followed the biblical Jesus until after his death. She was very close to him. After his death, she waited at his temporary burial place. She was the one who the biblical Jesus talked to after his resurrection: *"Jesus saith unto her, Mary. She turned herself, and saith unto him, Rabboni; which is to say, Master. Jesus saith unto her, Touch me not; for I am not yet ascended to my Fa-*

ther: but go to my brethren, and say unto them, I ascend unto my Father, and your Father; and to my God, and your God" (John, 20:16-17).

This biblical description is depicted in Tut-Ankh-Amen's tomb.

☞ There are striking similarities between Ankhsenpa-aton, Tut-Ankh-Amen's wife, and Mary Magdalene.

8

His Religion

Tut-Ankh-Amen

Tut-Ankh-Amen was a worshiper of Aton (Adonai in Hebrew) as per the following points (most of them were elaborated on, in earlier chapters).

1- The King's birth name was Tut-Ankh-**Aton** indicating his allegiance to Aton.

   His religion called for the worship of **Aton** - a supreme monotheistic God who had no image and as such would not manifest himself visually to his people. Aton is the God who became identified with the Hebrew Jehovah (the Lord), as Adonai.

2- His birth place, Amarna, was named after Amran (or Imran), which is the name of Akhenaton's god (father) and which is also the name given in the Bible for the father of the Jewish leader, Moses.

   Across the Nile from his birth place, is the city of Mal-Lawi (Mal-Levi), meaning *The City of the Levites*. The Levites are the people who, according to the Bible, held priestly positions with the Jewish leader, Moses. They are the very same people who held the same positions with Akhenaton (Tut's father) at Amarna.

3- The medical examination of his mummy, in 1968, confirmed that Tut had some Semitic features which he inherited from his great-grandfather, namely Yuya (identified in the Bible as the Israelite Joseph the Patriarch). The chapters under *The Family Roots* will explain his Semitic background.

4- Even though Tut changed his name from Tut-Ankh-**Aton** to Tut-Ankh-**Amen** in Year 4 of his reign, he still adhered completely to the Aton worship, as evident from his recovered throne. At the top center of his throne, one can see the symbol of the Aton, with its extending rays, giving the ankh, the Egyptian key of life, to Tut-Ankh-Amen and his wife. The Aton is represented here as the sole God. Two cartouches of Tut-Ankh-Amen are shown on the throne. One of these cartouches proves that he used this throne after he had changed his name.

5- *Aton Worship* (pages 112-116) provides the overwhelming evidence that the Jewish religious practices, rituals and history are mirror images of the Aton worship.

The Biblical Jesus

- The biblical Jesus was a worshiper of Adonai.
  "Think not that I have come to abolish the law and the prophets, I have come not to abolish them but to fulfil them." (Matthew, 5:17)

His Kingdom

9

Jesus, The King

To portray the biblical Jesus as an ordinary man of a humble family background, is to contradict the overwhelming evidence in the Bible itself that he was a monarch with power and authority. Here are some biblical references:

1- The Bible describes him as of royal blood, born *"King of the Jews"*. The Bible tells us that when Jesus was born, ***"wise men from the East came to Jerusalem, saying, "Where is he who has been born King of the Jews? ..."*** (Matthew, 2:2-3)

2- The Bible tells us that Herod, the King of Judea, was told of a prophecy that the biblical Jesus is to become, ***"... a ruler who will govern my people Israel."*** (Matthew, 2:6)
The biblical description of "a ruler to govern" leaves no doubt regarding his powerful role.

3- He was a man of authority, ***"And when Jesus finished these sayings, the crowds were astonished at his teachings, for he taught them as one who had authority, and not as their scribes."*** (Matthew, 7:28-29)

4- He was always addressed by the crowd as "Lord" on numerous occasions, signifying a person in a high position.

5- He showed his authority when he commanded his disciples to bring somebody else's ass and colt because *"The Lord has need of them."* *"... Jesus sent two disciples, saying to them, "Go into the village opposite you, and immediately you will find an ass tied, and a colt with her; untie them and bring them to me. If any one says anything to you, you shall say, 'The Lord has need of them'* (Matthew, 21:1-3)

6- The next biblical verses describe his role as the *King* of the Jews.
"Tell the daughter of Zion, Behold, your king is coming to you, humble, and mounted on an ass, and on a colt, the foal of an ass." (Matthew, 21:5) Also a very similar verse is stated in John, 12:13-15.

An Egyptian scene strikingly similar to the biblical verse.

7- The only question asked to him, indicates that he was the King, *"And Pilate asked him, "Are you the King of the Jews?" And he answered him, "You have said so."* (Mark, 15:2) Very similar verses are stated in Matthew, 27:11 and Luke, 23:3-4.

8- A short time later he again was referred to as the King, *"Hail, King of the Jews!"* (Matthew, 27:29)

9- Another reference to him as the King, *"And they began to salute him, "Hail, King of the Jews!"* (Mark, 15:18)

10- The charge against him which caused his execution was being the "King of the Jews", *"And over his head they put the charge against him, which read, "This is Jesus the King of the Jews."* (Matthew, 27:37) Also *"And the inscription of the charge against him read, "The King of the Jews."* (Mark, 15:26)

11- More references to him as the King, *"He is the King of Israel…"* (Matthew, 27:42) *"Let the Christ, the King of Israel…"* (Mark, 15:32) *"… and saying, "If you are the King of the Jews, save yourself!" There was also an inscription over him, "This is the King of the Jews."* (Luke, 23:37-38)

12- Here again he is called the King of the Jews, *"And he answered them, "Do you want me to release for you the King of the Jews?"* (Mark, 15:9)

13- Another reference to him as the King, *"And Pilate again said to them, "Then what shall I do with the man whom you call the King of the Jews?"* (Mark, 15:12)

14- He was the descendent of kings, *'Jesus Christ, the son* [meaning descendent] *of (King) David'* (Matthew, 1:1).

15- The Bible clearly states that Jesus inherited the throne of King David: ***"and the Lord God will give to him the throne of his father*** [meaning his ancestor] ***David."*** (Luke, 1:32)

16- He was addressed by ordinary people ***"Son of David"*** on numerous occassions throughout the Bible, which provides additional evidence that the historical Christ was of royal descent.

17- The joyous crowds are welcoming their king.

"So they took branches of palm trees and went out to meet him, crying, "Hosanna! Blessed is he who comes in the name of the Lord, even the King of Israel!" (John, 12:13)

An Egyptian Scene strikingly similar to the biblical verse (Palm Sunday)

✡ The Talmud agrees that:

1- Jesus was of royal descent, describing his mother as ***'the descendent of princes and rulers'*** (b. Sanh, 106a).

2- the biblical Jesus was in Egypt:

- ***"Jesus the Nazarene who practiced magic in Egypt"*** (b. Sanh., 107b).

10

The Divided Kingdom

In both cases of Tut-Ankh-Amen and the biblical Jesus, the evidence indicates a deep division in the kingdom.

Tut-Ankh-Amen

Akhenaton, King Tut's father, antagonized the populous and the priesthood by declaring Aton (Adonai in Hebrew) the only God, a God for the whole world. He shut down the temples of the other neteroo (gods) of Egypt, cut off financial support for them and sent the priests home.

Such actions caused a division in the kingdom between the Aton (Adonai) worshipers and the rest of the population.

After a few years of his tyranny, Akhenaton was forced to abdicate (more details later under the chapter, *The Tyrant Father*) and went into hiding with his followers to Sinai.

King Tut was ten years of age when he started his rule in 1361 B.C. At this young age, a custodian or guardian must have been in charge of the state affairs, as would be the case nowadays, if the legal heir is a minor.

- For four years he continued to live at Amarna, the capital city built by his father. There was no change in the state of affairs as left by Akhenaton.

- After four years, he recognized and accepted the fact that the majority of his people did not share his own beliefs. To reconcile the different views in his kingdom, Tut:
  1- Re-opened the other Egyptian temples and the other neteroo (gods) were recognized again.
  2- Changed his name from Tut-Ankh-**Aton** to Tut-Ankh-**Amen**. The change was in recognition of Amen.

☞ Tut never changed his religious beliefs, as evident from his recovered throne. The Aton is represented on the throne as the sole God.

The Biblical Jesus

Here are some of the clear biblical references to the division in his kingdom, as he addressed the Adonai worshipers:

1- *"... he said to them, "Every kingdom divided against itself is laid waste, and no city or house divided against itself will stand; and if Satan casts out Satan, he is divided against himself; how then will his kingdom stand?"* (Matthew, 12:25-26)

2- *"If a kingdom is divided against itself, that kingdom cannot stand. And if a house is divided against itself, that house will not be able to stand."* (Mark, 3:24-25)

3- *"But he, knowing their thoughts, said to them, "Every kingdom divided against itself is laid waste, and house falls upon house."* (Luke, 11:17)

11

Quest for Unification

Tut-Ankh-Amen

In his Year 9, Tut-Ankh-Amen, accompanied by his uncle Aye, went to Sinai to try to urge Akhenaton and his followers to return to Egypt. He wanted them to live in harmony with people of different beliefs whom they regarded as enemies. His repeated message was reconciliation, forgiveness and tolerance. Unlike his father, he accepted that not everyone had the same perception of God and not everyone worshiped him in the same way. Live and let live.
Instead of his pleas being accepted, he was accused of betraying his faith and was killed.

The Biblical Jesus

Similarly, the biblical Jesus went solely to bring back the Adonai/Aton followers:
"These twelve (disciples) Jesus sent out, charging them, "Go nowhere among the Gentiles, and enter no town of the Samaritans, but go rather to the lost sheep of the house of Israel." (Matthew, 10:5-6)
Like Tut, his message was also reconciliation, forgiveness and tolerance. His message was very clear in his Sermon on the Mount, portions of which are mentioned herein.

1- *"Blessed are the peacemakers, for they shall be called Sons of God."* (Matthew, 5:9)

2- *"Think not that I have come to abolish the law and the prophets, I have come not to abolish them but to fulfil them."* (Matthew, 5:17)

3- *"But if you do not forgive men their trespasses neither will your Father forgive your trespasses."* (Matthew, 6:15)

4- *"But I say to you that hear, Love your enemies, do good to those who hate you, bless those who curse you, pray for those who abuse you. To him who strikes you on the cheek, offer the other also; and from him who takes away your cloak do not withhold your coat as well. Give to every one who begs from you; and of him who takes away your goods do not ask them again. And as you wish that men would do to you, do so to them."* (Luke, 6:27-31)

5- *"Judge not, and you will not be judged; condemn not, and you will not be condemned; forgive, and you will be forgiven; give, and it will be given to you; good measure, pressed down, shaken together, running over, will be put into your lap. For the measure you give will be the measure you get back."* (Luke, 6:37-38)

☞ Similarly, his pleas were not accepted. Instead he was accused of betraying his faith — and was killed.

12

Death in the Wilderness

Tut-Ankh-Amen

• The violent nature of Tut-Ankh-Amen's death is evident from the condition of his mummy. An extensive examination of Tut's mummy, including the use of x-rays, was carried out in 1968. The mummy was found to have many broken bones and joints. The tissues of the face were contracted. The teeth were tightly clenched together. There was no evidence of disease as the cause of death. The final conclusion was that he did not die of natural causes, but that he suffered from physical torture before he was hanged.

• The funerary mask of Tut-Ankh-Amen, the best likeness of a pharaoh ever found, shows the suffering eyes of the young King, at his death.

• Howard Carter reported that he found many items in Tut-Ankh-Amen's tomb that linked them *"to later Christian beliefs and practices"*, such as:

a- His scepter which was used in conjunction with offerings. It contains this text: 'The Beautiful God, beloved, dazzling of face like the Aton when it shines ... Tut-Ankh-Amen.'

✞ The text is very similar to the biblical accounts of the Transfiguration of Jesus and his *"shining face"* on the Mount shortly before he died.

b- Fruits and seeds of Christ-thorn, a tree like a hawthorn, native to ancient Egypt, used for food or medicine, and also said to have had some religious significance.

✞ These thorny shrubs said to have been used for Christ's crown of thorns: *'And the soldiers plaited a crown of thorns, and put it on his head . . .'* (John, 19:2).

c- Two ritual robes.

✞ Carter identified them as the "same priestly dalmatic worn by Christian deacons and bishops."

• The botanical evidence found in the tomb shows that Tut-Ankh-Amen must have died in the spring and was buried seventy days later, the time required for the mummification process. Spring blossoms and fruits were found in wreaths, on top of the second and third coffins. These must have been dried out before use. The wreath on the third coffin included the mandrake fruits, sliced in half which were dried out before they were sewn on to the wreath. Additionally, the blue water-lily used in these wreaths does not bloom until the summer.

Tut-Ankh-Amen most probably died in April, the same time as the biblical Christ's death.

The Biblical Jesus

1- How Did He Die?

There are conflicting accounts of how Jesus died.

✞ The New Testament claims that Jesus was crucified:

- *"And they crucified him ..."* (Matthew, 27:35)
- *"And when they had crucified him ..."* (Mark, 15:24)
- *"And when they were come to the place, which is called Calvary, there they crucified him ..."* (Luke, 23:33)
- *"Then the soldiers, when they had crucified Jesus ..."* (John, 19:23).
- Paul stated: *"... Jesus, whom ye have crucified ..."* (Acts, 2:36).

☞ However, crucifixion was a Roman, not an Israelite, form of execution. This form of execution would be expected had Jesus been tried and condemned by a Roman court, which was never the case. He was sentenced to death by the Jewish heirarchy. The Israelites hanged the condemned person from a tree: *"And if a man have committed a sin worthy of death ... thou hang him on a tree"* (Deuteronomy, 21:22).

✞ There are also references in the New Testament to Jesus being hanged, as per the following accounts by Peter:

- *"... Jesus, whom ye slew and hanged on a tree"* (Acts, 5:30)
- *"And we are witnesses to all that he did both in the country of the Jews and in Jerusalem. They put him*

to death by hanging him on a tree ..." (Acts, 10:39)

- *"... they took him down from the tree, and laid him in a tomb"* (Acts, 13:29).

✡ The Old Testament states that Jesus was hanged from a tree, *'His body shall not remain all night upon the tree, but thou shalt in any wise bury him that day; (for he that is hanged is accursed of God) ...'* (Deuteronomy, 21:23).

✡ The Talmud refers to Jesus as having been

a- crucified:
"It seems that the king [Jesus] is crucified" (T. Sanh., 9.7).

b- hanged:
"Jesus was hanged" (b. Sanh., 106b)
"They hanged him on the eve of the Passover" (b. Sanh., 43a).

✞ As a result, it could be that *crucifixion* and *hanging* are not contradicting but synonymous, in this case.

2- Who Condemned Him? and Why?

✞ The New Testament tells us that Jesus was wary of the Jewish priesthood. In Matthew, 23, for example, there are numerous accusations against them. Many biblical verses in Matthew, 23 begins with *"Woe to you scribes and Pharisees, hypocrites! For you ...* (accusations)*"*

✞ The New Testament clearly and totally blames the Israelite priests for condemning him to death. He was at variance with the Jewish heirachy. Their charge against him was blasphemy of the Jewish Scripts. The Bible did not indicate any charge against him by the Romans whatsoever:

1- *"... the Son of man shall be betrayed unto the chief priests and unto the scribes, and they shall condemn him to death"* (Matthew, 20:18)

2- *"The Jews answered him, "We have a law, and by that law he ought to die, because he has made himself the Son of God."* (John, 19:7)

   ☞ *Son of God* was the title of all Egyptian kings since ca. 3000 B.C.

3- Peter pointed to the Jerusalem priests: *"... Jesus, whom ye slew and hanged on a tree"* (Acts, 5:30)

4- Paul said *"the Jews, who killed the Lord Jesus"* (I Thessalonians, 2:14-15).

5- *"Then the high priest tore his robes, and said, "He has uttered blasphemy. Why do we still need witnesses? You have now heard his blasphemy. What is your judgement?" They answered, "He deserves death." Then they spat in his face, and struck him; and some slapped him, saying, "Prophesy to us, you Christ! Who is it that struck you?"* (Matthew, 26:65-68)

6- A very similar situation to the above Matthew, 26:65-

68 is described in Mark, 14:61-65.

7- *"When morning came, all the chief priests and the elders took counsel against Jesus to put him to death;"* (Matthew, 27:1)

8- *"And Pilate asked him, "Are you the King of the Jews?" And he answered him, "You have said so." And Pilate said to the chief priests and the multitudes, "I find no crime in this man."* (Luke, 23:3-4)

9- *"Pilate then called together the chief priests and the rulers of the people, and said to them, "You brought me this man as one who was perverting the people; and after examining him before you, behold, I did not find this man guilty of any of your charges against him; neither did Herod, for he sent him back to us. Behold, nothing deserving death has been done by him; I will therefore chastise him and release him."* (Luke, 23:13-16)

10- *"Pilate said to them, "Take him yourselves and judge him by your own law." The Jews said to him, "It is not lawful for us to put any man to death."* (John, 18:31) This biblical verse is contrary to *"And if a man have committed a sin worthy of death ... thou hang him on a tree"* (Deuteronomy, 21:22) as well as *"The Jews answered him, "We have a law, and by that law he ought to die, because he has made himself the Son of God."* (John, 19:7)

11- *"he* (Pilate) *went out to the Jews again, and told*

them, "I find no crime in him." (John, 18:38)

12- *"Pilate went out again, and said to them, "Behold, I am bringing him out to you, that you may know that I find no crime in him."* (John, 19:4)

3- Who Killed Him?

✞ The New Testament identifies the Jews as the killers.

1- *"... The Jews, who killed both the Lord Jesus and the prophets, and drove us out, and displease God and oppose all men ..."* (I Thessalonians, 2:14-15)

2- The biblical accounts that the Jewish crowd insisted on killing him, is contrary to the content of the biblical verse *"And as they led him away, ... And there followed him a great multitude of the people, and of women who bewailed and lamented him."* (Luke, 23:26-27)

✡ The Talmud clearly identifies Jesus' killer as Pinhas, the Israelite priest who lived in the fourteenth century B.C. and was a companion of Moses. The rabbis accepted that the Israelite priests were responsible for the condemnation of Jesus as a punishment for his having led Israel astray. The Jewish rabbis never mention additional involvement of Pontius Pilate or the Romans in the circumstances surrounding his death.

- *'... they hanged Jesus (the Nazarene) ... because he hath practised magic and deceived and led astray Israel'* (b. Sanh., 43a).

- The Talmud is quite specific: *'Pinhas ... killed him [Jesus]'* (b. Sanh., 106b). Pinhas (Phinehas, to use the name shown in the Old Testament) was the priest, the son of Eleazar, the son of Aaron, who is identified in the Book of Numbers as a contemporary of Moses.

Phinehas looked upon Jesus' teachings of religious co-existence as blasphemy. On the eve of the Passover, Pinhas/Phinehas killed Jesus in the Tabernacle at the foot of Mount Sinai.

Aye (Ephraim), the second son of Joseph the Patriarch, and Tut-Ankh-Amen's successor, killed thousands of Israelites, including Pinhas/Phinehas as a punishment for Jesus' death.

St. Catherine Monastery, built in the 6th century A.D., nestled at the foot of Mount Sinai, where Tut/Jesus was hung from a tree.

13

Resurrection & Easter

Tut-Ankh-Amen

• As explained in earlier chapters, the evidence from King Tut's tomb proves that he died in the spring time. Such a time coincided with an ancient Egyptian holiday.

• More than five thousand years ago, ancient Egyptians adopted a national holiday, which came at the end of a four day ceremony. According to Egyptian legend, Osiris died, was buried and then disappeared on Friday. They called that day the *Loss of Osiris*. Osiris was resurrected on the third day, i.e. on Sunday, as the judge (king) of the dead. The fourth day was and is the day of festivities.

Osiris was associated with both the lunar and solar cycles. The four day ceremony of the death and resurrection of Osiris was therefore held at the end of the first week following the full moon (lunar cycle), following the vernal equinox (solar cycle), which is exactly the same date that was later set for the Christian Easter.

Osiris

Like the biblical Jesus:

- Osiris symbolizes the divine in a mortal form.

• Osiris symbolizes mortal man carrying within himself the potential for spiritual salvation.

• The Egyptian King embodied the personal, spiritual destiny of all mankind. In death, the Egyptian King was assimilated to the mortal neter (god), Osiris.
The dead King was equated with Osiris, and since the King represented all men, all men in death were Osiris.
Isis held a similar role with women.

• Easter Monday is and has been a national holiday in Egypt, for at least five thousand years. It is called the "Breath of Life" day. It is the happiest day in the Egyptian calendar. People shed their winter clothes and wear their brightest outfits. Uniformed officers store their black wool uniforms, and don their white outfits.

• One of the best-known Easter symbols is the egg, which has symbolized renewed life since ancient times, because all living creatures begin life in the egg. Egyptians continue to color eggs and eat them during their celebration.

The Biblical Jesus

• The biblical Jesus (like King Tut) died also in the spring time. His death and Resurrection were observed later as the Easter celebration.

• The Webster's dictionary describes Easter as *"name of pagan vernal festival almost coincident in date with paschal festival of the church".* The so-called *pagan* festival is the Egyptian Easter.

• As is the case of the Egyptian Easter, the Christian Easter is always celebrated at the end of the first week after the full moon, following the vernal equinox (when day and night are of equal length in the spring). The date of Easter Sunday was established by the Church Council of Nicaea in A.D. 325.

• As is the case of the Egyptian Osiris, the Christian Easter reflects the Christian conviction that Christ died, was buried, and subsequently disappeared on Friday, and was resurrected the third day after his death, i.e. on Sunday. It is the happiest day in the Christian calendar.

• The biblical Jesus believed in life after death, which Moses never spoke of. When the Jews were getting ready to execute the biblical Jesus, the Jews mocked him and challenged him to come back from the dead.

☞ The account of the Resurrection of Jesus in many ways is similar to that of Osiris. Like Osiris, he is said to have risen on the third day. The Osiris worshippers of ancient Egypt believed, as did the early Christians (Hebrews, 4:14), that ***"man cannot be saved"*** by a distant Almighty, but by one who has shared the experience of human suffering and death.
  - Both Osiris and Jesus suffered and died.
  - Both became the savior to whom men and women turned, for assurance of immortality.

☞ The medieval Passion plays concerning the death and Resurrection of Jesus closely parallels the death and Resurrection of the Egyptian King as Osiris.

☞ As you can see, the Christian Easter is a mirror image of the Egyptians' Breath of Life celebration, except for one major difference: the Gospels' tale of Jesus' death and resurrection is considered historical and the ancient Egyptian tale of Osiris is spiritual in a legendary form.

Cover Up

14

Nazarenes The Gnostic Sect

It is an error to think that ***Jesus the Nazarene*** means Jesus from a city named Nazareth located in Galilee.

☞ The name Nazareth is **not found** in:

- The Book of Acts
- The letters of the Apostles
- Any book of the Old Testament
- The Talmud
- The whole works of the Jewish historian Josephus, who was himself given command in Galilee at the time of the Jewish revolt against the Romans in 66 A.D.

☞ The English version of the New Testament always and incorrectly translated the word *Nazarene* as *of Nazareth*.

☞ The Talmud never mentions that Jesus was a Galilean or came from the city of Nazareth. The Talmud refers to him as being a Nazarene (Greek, Nazaraious) indicating a religious sect, not a geographical location.

☞ Paul, himself always referred to Jesus as 'the Nazarene' and never mentions that he came from Nazareth.

Nazarenes signifies a religious sect and not a geographical location, as per the following biblical verses:

1- *"For we have found this man* (Paul) *a pestilent fellow, an agitator among all the Jews throughout the world, and a ringleader of the sect of the Nazarenes."* (Acts, 24:5)

2- *"But this I admit to you, that according to the Way, which they call a sect, I worship the God of our fathers, believing everything laid down by the law or written in the prophets ..."* (Acts, 24:14)

☥ The Nazarenes were one of many Gnostic sects (seekers of knowledge through spiritual experience). Hebrew Jews, to this day, use the term *Nazarene* for Christians.

15

The Cover-Up Scheme

The killing of the biblical Jesus was always remembered by those who believed in him and later became his followers. The Jewish priesthood, however, deliberately concealed both his killing and its date. Here is how they did it.

Concealing His Death

Originally, both the Day of Atonement (Yom Kippur) and Passover were observed as one feast in the month of Abib (Babylonian Nisan), in the spring time. Two major changes occurred:

1- The Day of Atonement is now observed in autumn and not in spring.

2- The significance of the Day of Atonement changed from a day of repentance, for the killing of the Messiah, to become a day for general repentance for sin.

Let us backtrack through this cover-up scheme.

1- After Moses left Egypt, he and his followers observed the feast of the Passover: *"Thou shalt keep the feast of unleavened bread: (thou shalt eat unleavened bread seven days... in the time appointed of the month Abib (Nisan); for in it thou camest out from Egypt ...)"* (Exodus,

23:15). The Passover is originally an Egyptian spring festival, which was observed for seven days, from the fifteenth to the twenty-first day of Abib (Babylonian Nisan). This was also the first month of the Israelite year.
After Jesus died, on the eve of the Passover, the fourteenth day of Abib, the Israelites offered a sacrificial lamb in atonement for the killing of Jesus: ***"Thou shalt therefore sacrifice the Passover unto the Lord thy God, of the flock and the herd... thou shalt sacrifice the Passover at even [evening], at the going down of the sun, at the season that thou camest forth out of Egypt"*** (Deuteronomy, 16:2,6).

2- The Jewish sect, the Essenes, took the view that they had nothing to feel guilty about and regarded Christ as their sacrificial lamb. On the same day, the fourteenth day of Abib, the Essenes held a Messianic Banquet awaiting the return of their dead, Teacher of Righteousness, at the end of the world, when he would celebrate the meal with them. This Messianic Banquet is very similar to the Last Supper.

3- Later Christians stopped the practice of animal sacrifice because they regarded Jesus himself as the sacrifice: ***"For even the Son of a man came not to be ministered unto, but to minister, and to give his life a ransom for many"*** (Mark, 10:45) and ***"... Behold the Lamb of God, which taketh away the sins of the world"*** (John, 1:29).

4- During the Babylonian exile, in the sixth century B.C., the Jewish priests wrote the Books of the Pentateuch, which had originated at the time of Moses. They referred to the date of the Passover as either *the first month* or as *Nisan*.

The Jewish priests replaced, in exile, the solar calendar, used previously, with the Babylonian lunar calendar. As a result, Tishri (September - October), which was the seventh month of the Israelites' year, became the first month of a new calendar.

To manage the confusion caused by the calendar change, Ezekiel divided the year into two parts with the religious observances of the first month repeated in the seventh.

After the Jews' return from Babylon, their priests stopped the practice of two annual observations of the same event. This was the most opportune time to separate Atonement Day (in autumn) from Passover (in spring).

5- Splitting one event (Passover and Day of Atonement) into two separate events was followed by changing the significance of the Day of Atonement from a day of repentance, for killing the Messiah, to become a day for general repentance for sin.

It became increasingly interesting when the Bible stated that the Messiah (the victim) was an Egyptian pharaoh, and that the *Lord* was his executioner: ***"The Lord smote ... the firstborn of Pharaoh that sat on his throne..."*** (Exodus, 12:29).

☞ The Book of Exodus, as such, has confirmed that the executed victim, at the foot of Mount Sinai, on the day Jesus died, was an Egyptian King whose father was still alive.

If it was simply the firstborn of a ruling pharaoh who was smitten, there is no reason to add the words ***"that sat on his throne"***. Therefore the biblical verse confirms that there was another pharaoh who was not sitting on his throne.

Unintentionally, they left the evidence that the victim was none other than Tut-Ankh-Amen (Jesus) who sat on his father's, Akhenaton (the historical Moses), throne. Akhenaton was still alive, hiding in Sinai. Read more details in the chapter, *The Tyrant Father*.

A Fabricated Time and Place

- The Essenes (the followers of Essa/Jesus) worked secretly for centuries to keep the memory of their Teacher of Righteousness alive, until his return (second coming).

- When John the Baptist lived and died many centuries later, the Essene leaders who had been waiting for the Second Coming of Christ, thought that John was the Messiah.

  "As the people were in expectation, and all men questioned in their hearts concerning John, whether perhaps he were the Christ ..." (Luke, 3:15)

- The evangelists (the writers of the Gospels) chose to ignore the Essenes' belief in John the Baptist, as the Second Coming of Christ, and elected to use the time period and the place where John the Baptist lived, to tell the story of Jesus Christ, as his First Coming. This led to the evangelists adopting the time of Herod the Great and Pontious Pilate for the birth and life of Jesus.

☞ The secrecy surrounding the hidden contents of the Dead Sea Scrolls is another clear indication that the cover-up is still continuing.

The Family Roots

16

His Royal Family

To reinforce the evidence that Tut-Ankh-Amen and the biblical Jesus are one and the same, let us retrace their family roots.

Tut-Ankh-Amen

Kings of the Later Eighteenth Dynasty

King	*Length of reign*	*Dates*	
Tuthmosis III (DAVID)	54	1490-1436 B.C.	
Amenhotep II	23	1436-1413 B.C.	
Tuthmosis IV	8	1413-1405 B.C.	
Amenhotep III (SOLOMON)	38	1405-1367 B.C.	
Akhenaton (MOSES) (alone and with Semenkhare)	6	1367-1361 B.C.	Amarna Kings
Semenkhkare	-	1361-1361 B.C.	Amarna Kings
Tut-Ankh-Amen (JESUS)	9	1361-1352 B.C.	Amarna Kings
Aye (EPHRAIM)	4	1352-1348 B.C.	Amarna Kings
Horemheb	13	1348-1335 B.C.	

These dates vary from other known lists.
The difference, between them and other lists, will be resolved in the coming chapters, when the co-regency periods between some kings are clarified.

The Biblical Jesus

As mentioned earlier, Jesus has been called *Son* (meaning

ancestor) *of David*, numerous times. In Chapter 1 of the Gospel According to Matthew, the biblical Jesus is shown to be the descendent of:

1- King David
2- King Solomon
3- Moses

In order for David to be Jesus' ancestor he must have preceded both Jesus and Moses and not followed them.
The biblical David is thought to have lived in the tenth century B.C. If the historical Jesus was a contemporary of Moses and lived and died in Sinai in the fourteenth century B.C., how could David, who followed Jesus, be his ancestor?!!

This logical conclusion can only be affirmed in the Egyptian records. Not only is the biblical chronology illogical, there is also a total lack of historical evidence to support the biblical accounts of these very important characters.

Matching the Family Roots

While there is no historical evidence to support the biblical accounts of David, Solomon and Moses, there is abundant evidence to prove that:

- **Moses' life and religion match precisely with those of King Akhenaton (1367-1361 B.C.).**
- **King David's war accounts match precisely with those of King Tuthomosis III (1490-1436 B.C.).**
- **King Solomon's life and lack of wars match precisely with those of King Amenhotep III (1436-1413 B.C.).**

Please have an open mind.

17

The Mighty Great^3-Grandfather

Tuthomosis III *(David)*

The Name

T•W•T / D•W•D

Since the ancient language didn't have short vowels, the first element of this king's name was always written as *Twt*, i.e. with three consonants. For some mischievous reasons, the middle consonant letter was changed to the vowel *u*, by some Egyptologists. When *Twt* is written, in the equivalent Hebrew alphabetical characters, it becomes *Dwd*. When *Dwd* is pronounced phonetically it becomes *Dawood* which is the Hebrew name for *David.*

Is there any chance that the Egyptian warrior king was actually the biblical warrior King David? Let us study the accounts of the Egyptian David (Tuthomosis III) and the biblical David.

The life of the biblical David can be divided into two parts:

I As a youth rising into prominence among his people. (We shall prove that the biblical account of his youth was borrowed from an ancient Egyptian tale and that the biblical account is historically baseless.)

II As a warrior king of his people. (We shall prove that basically the biblical war accounts of King David match precisely the war accounts of Tuthomosis III.)

(I) His Youth

✡ **Biblical Account**
David, who supposedly lived in the first half of the tenth century B.C., was the youngest son of Jesse. As a young boy he was a shepherd and a harpist. He was introduced to Saul, who appointed him as his armorbearer. Goliath, who was a huge, armored and strong giant, came from the Philistine camp to intimidate the Israelites, by challenging them to a man-to-man contest. Goliath had a strong iron spear, sword and a shield. Goliath asked the Israelites to choose an opponent and promised: *"If he be able to fight with me, and kill me, then we will be your servants."* David volunteered to fight Goliath but Saul tried to persuade him otherwise. Then David told Saul: *"Thy servant kept his father sheep, and there came a lion, and a bear, and took a lamb out of the flock: And I went out after him, and smote him, and delivered it out of his mouth: and when he rose against me, I caught him by his beard, and smote him, and slew him. Thy servant slew both the lion and the bear. . . . The Lord has delivered me out of the paw*

of the lion, and out of the paw of the bear, he will deliver me out of the hand of the Philistine." (I Samuel 17:34-37)

David refused to wear armor or carry a sword and went to face Goliath; David then knocked Goliath down with a stone from his sling and took Goliath's sword and cut off his head. The Bible tells us then, *"David took the head of the Philistine (Goliath) and brought it to Jerusalem, but he put his armor in his tent."* (I Samuel, 17:54)

☥Historical Analysis of the Biblical Account

1- The Bible tells us that Goliath was a Philistine (which is the same as Palestinian). But when did these Philistines settle and establish themselves in Canaan?
The archaeological evidence indicates that the Philistines became an established community only after the reign of Ramses III (c. 1182-1151 B.C.), as per:

a- The walls of Ramses III's funerary temple in western Thebes depict the mass invasion by the *Peoples of the Sea*, of the coastal plain of Canaan, around 1174 B.C., which coincided with the Greek war against Troy. The wall inscriptions also indicate that the Peoples of the Sea were a combination of Peleset (which are Palestinians/Philistines - the word *Palestine* came from *Peleset*), Tjekker, Sheklesh, Danu and Weshesh. The walls of this temple also depict the fact that the invading people were after permanent settlement, for they consisted of whole families. Ramses III defeated the invaders in a naval battle and many of the captives were allowed to settle in southwest Canaan.

b- The Harris Papyrus, in the British Museum, states that Ramses III built a temple for Amen in Canaan after he defeated the invaders.

It was only after the reign of Ramses III, that Egypt lost control over Palestine, and the Philistines established themselves in the coastal plains of Canaan. Then they started expanding towards the Dead Sea and the River Jordan. It was at the same time, that the Israelites were trying to establish themselves in the area. Because of the vacuum left after the reign of Ramses III, both Philistines and Israelites began fighting over the same piece of land.

☞ Historically speaking, if David did do battle with the Philistines, he could not have lived before the twelfth century B.C., because that was when the mass invasion of the coastal plain of Canaan by the Philistines took place. Therefore, historical facts contradict the biblical time period of the David and Goliath duel, to occur during the first half of the tenth century.

2- The Bible, in the Second Book of Samuel, speaks of Goliath as having been born to the giants. The Raphaim (giants) and the Philistines are totally different people who lived in two different eras.

3- The biblical account of David and Goliath occurred, according to the Book of Samuel, when Jerusalem was not yet under Israelite control. Why and how did David take Goliath's head to a foreign city under enemy's control?! ***"David took the head of the Philistine (Goliath), and brought it to Jerusalem, but he put his armor in his tent."*** (I Samuel, 17:54)

4- Many scholars have noted the mirror image similarities between the most famous ancient Egyptian tale The Autobiography of Sinuhe and the biblical account of David and Goliath.

William Kelly Simpson wrote, *"The account of the fight between the champion of Retenu (Sinuhe) has frequently been compared to the David and Goliath duel, for which it may have served as a literary prototype."*

Sinuhe and the Giant

☥ The Sinuhe tale existed in many ancient Egyptian texts as far back as the twentieth century B.C. Therefore, it was in existence a thousand years before the biblical account of David and Goliath was supposed to have occurred.

☥ Sinuhe's opponent in the famous tale, was a giant. Giant people were said to have lived in Canaan around the twentieth century B.C., when this tale was first developed.

✡ The Israelites, during their sojourn in Egypt, must have been influenced by the very popular Egyptian Sinuhe tale.

Based on all the above, the story of David and Goliath is a fictional story which was inserted in the Bible in an attempt to enhance the biblical King David's trait as a

hero and a warrior, and that the events of the duel between David and Goliath were actually borrowed from the Egyptian literary work The Autobiography of Sinuhe.

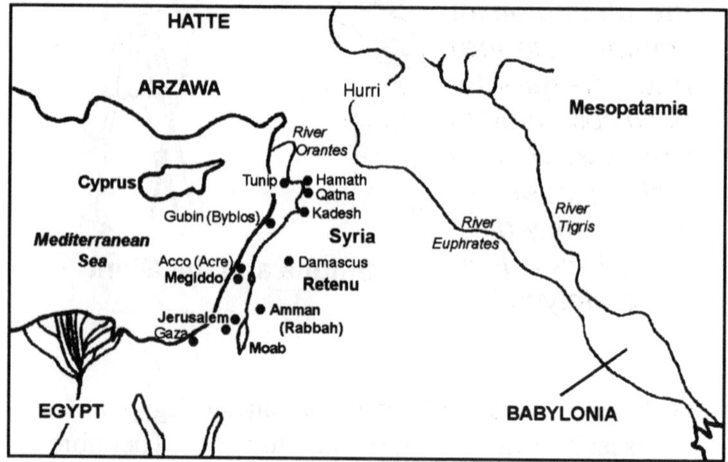

The Empire between the Nile and the Euphrates

(II) The Warrior King

✡ The Biblical Warrior King

Shortly after the David and Goliath event, David was suddenly transformed into a mighty warrior. The biblical accounts of the campaigns fought by David are described in the Second Book of Samuel. It shows an account of a series of wars in northern Palestine, Syria (up to the limits of the Mesopotamian river, the Euphrates) as well as Moab, to the east of the Dead Sea.

A few discrepancies in his biblical campaigns need to be discussed and clarified.

A- Confused Chronology

1- The Bible tells us that David defeated the confederate Syrian Kingdom, which was led by Hadadezer. ***'David slayed twenty thousand of them, put garrisons in Aram of Damascus, and the Syrians became his servants and paid tribute.'***

   The second book of Samuel (8:3) specifically tells us that David ***"smote also Hadadezer... King of Zobath*** (located near Hamath in northern Syria), ***as he went to recover his border at the river Euphrates."***

2- Two biblical chapters later, however, in describing David's campaign against the Ammonites, we find the Syrians and Zobath (who were just totally wiped out) are fighting David!

   We are now told that the Ammonites were asking the Syrians for military support (!) and that Zobath (the defeated city) was among the Syrian allies (!)

   We are also told that after David defeated the Ammonites' allies, they fled and sought refuge in their city, Rabbah (present-day Amman, the capital city of Jordan), and that David's army returned to besiege Rabbah.

☞ • **This situation is impossible, if Zobath had already been defeated and David had established garrisons in Syria.**

☞ • **Geographically and logically, these two events must have taken place chronologically in the reverse order to that described in the biblical account.**

B- Confused City-Names

1- Rabbah- is present-day Amman, the capital city of Jordan. The Bible claims that David conquered Rabbah after a long siege in the first half of the tenth century B.C. However, no archaeological evidence was ever found to support that claim.

☞ The biblical editor made a mistake in naming *Rabbah* as the city, besieged and attacked by David. The correct name is *Megiddo*.
The Bible itself disputes the validity of the Rabbah story.

a- The military importance of Megiddo and its legend, as an international battleground, is reflected in John (Revelation, 16:16). **Armageddon (*Har Meggiddon*, the Mount of Megiddo)** is the site where, at the end of days, all the kings of the world will fight the ultimate battle against the forces of God.

b- In the second book of Samuel (10:2), we are told that David took the city of Rabbah, whose king was Hanun. Seven chapters later, we find Rabbah independent under its king, Shobi, who felt pity on David and his followers because they were ***"hungry and weary, and thirsty in the wilderness."*** (II Samuel, 17:28-9)

Rabbah was a minor insignificant location at that time.

c- Solomon, David's successor, who inherited the empire without war, raised a levy so as ***"to build the wall of Megiddo."*** (I Kings 9:15)

d- **Megiddo** is also mentioned as one of Solomon's possessions in I Kings, 4:12.

2- Zobath- No traces of a locality with this name have been found in either Syria or Canaan at the supposed time of David (tenth century B.C.) or Tuthomosis III (fifteenth century B.C.).

☞ Zobath was mistaken for the city of Qadesh, the northern Syrian stronghold, on the River Orontes.

☥ The Egyptian Warrior King

When Tuthomosis III became the sole ruler of Egypt, after the death of Hatshepsut, four decades had passed without a major Egyptian military campaign in western Asia. During this period, the Syrian King of Qadesh led a Syria-Canaanite confederacy in a general rebellion against the Egyptian presence, which was secured since the reign of Tuthomosis I (c. 1528-1510 B.C.).

In response to the rebellion, Tuthomosis III led a total of seventeen campaigns in western Asia over the next twenty years. The daily events of these wars fought by Tuthomosis III, were recorded by the scribes who accompanied the army on its campaigns. These records are to be found in the Annals, a 223-line document that covers the inside of the walls enclosing the corridor surrounding the granite holy of holies, which Tuthomosis III built at the Karnak temple.

☞ **The historical details of the wars fought by the Warrior King Tuthomosis III, in the Karnak temple, match precisely the biblical accounts of the wars fought by the Warrior King David, in the second book of Samuel, except for the discrepancies in the chronology of a single event and the two city names, mentioned earlier.**

The common denominator of the events at the biblically named Rabbah and the Egyptian named Megiddo, as evident from both the war annals of Tuthomosis III and the biblical account of David's campaigns, are:

* The king fought against a major fortified city in Canaan that was aided by a Syrian confederation led by a king of one Syrian city;

* The king's army defeated the coalition near the city gates and the enemy sought sanctuary within its fortified walls;

* The king's army surrounded the city for a long time before they attacked it and took it;

* After the defeat of the Syrian confederation at (Rabbah/Megiddo), the main Syrian city went on threatening the king. The king and his army therefore conquered that Syrian city and went further to regain the borders at the River Euphrates. He then erected a stele in celebration of his triumph.

☞ **Historical and archaeological evidence confirms that these military campaigns occurred during the reign of Tuthomosis III. There is no evidence to support the biblical account that these events occurred five centuries later, at the supposed time of the biblical David in the first half of the tenth century B.C.**

18

The Weak Grandfather

Amenhotep III *(Solomon)*

General

☞ The evidence points to Amenhotep III, as being the historical figure of the person identified in the Old Testament as Solomon. This evidence is described below. The actions, or lack thereof, of Amenhotep III, which rendered him as a weak king (figure head), will be very obvious in the next chapter.

☥ Thirty-two years after the death of the warrior King Tuthomosis III, his great-grandson, Amenhotep III, sat upon the throne of Egypt.

King	Length of Reign	Dates
Tuthomosis III (David)	54	1490-1436 B.C.
Amenhotep II	23	1436-1413 B.C.
Tuthomosis IV	8	1413-1405 B.C.
Amenhotep III (Solomon)	38	1405-1367 B.C.

Egypt was the universal leader of the known world with a vast empire between the Nile and Euphrates. Amenhotep III later became known as *'king of kings,*

ruler of rulers ...'
Amenhotep III's reign was almost entirely peaceful except for a minor military operation in northern Sudan, during Year 5 of his reign. He developed alliances and diplomatic ties between himself and other leaders of the then-known world, to create a peaceful international climate. The name Solomon means *safety* or *peace*.

✡ Solomon, according to the Old Testament, followed David to the throne at Jerusalem. Biblical scholars have assigned c. 965-925 B.C. as the dates of Solomon's forty-year reign. The peaceful conditions of Amenhotep III's reign were also attributed to the biblical Solomon.

☞ There is no historical record of a ruler named Solomon at any time. Furthermore, both the Old Testament and the Talmud agree that Solomon was not the king's original name. According to II Samuel 12:25, at the time of his birth, the prophet Nathan gave Solomon the name of Jedidiah, meaning ***'because of the Lord'*** or ***'by the word of the Lord'***.

☥ Coronation of the King ✡

☥ Amenhotep III, as the King of Egypt, was regarded as the son of the deity. This is an exclusively ancient Egyptian concept, applying to all their kings.

✡ The idea of kingship, originally foreign to the Hebrews, was introduced into the Israelite theology from the time of David onward. In their case, as in Egyptian tradition, the king is regarded as the son of the deity. Jehovah tells King David in Psalms 2:7, ***"Thou art my son; this day have I begotten thee."*** He also says of Solomon, ***"I will***

be his father, and he shall be my son" (II Samuel, 7:14)

• • •

☥ Anointing the king was an ancient Egyptian (beginning ~ 2700 B.C.), not a Hebrew custom.

✡ According to the Bible, David ordered Solomon to be anointed ***'king over Israel'*** (I Kings, 1:34). Like the Egyptians, the Israelite Lord began referring to his kingly son as ***"his anointed"***. (Psalms, 2:2, 18:50, 20:6)
The Hebrew word **'MeSHeH'**, meaning *the anointed one*, is borrowed from the Egyptian word **'MeSSeH'** meaning the same thing.

• • •

☥ The German biblical scholar Otto Eissfeldt describing the throne of the biblical Solomon stated, *"It is comparatively easy to visualize the throne of gold and ivory with its six steps which stood in the audience chamber as it is described in I Kings, (11:11-20) ... The lavish use of gold can be compared without hesitation with the wonderfully-preserved chair of Tut-Ankh-Amen."* Tut-Ankh-Amen was Amenhotep III's grandson.

✡ After Solomon was anointed, David said that Solomon should come and ***'sit upon my throne'*** (I Kings, 1:35).

☞ The mirror image similarity between the biblical description of Solomon's throne and the actual throne of Tut-Ankh-Amen, cannot be coincidental.

☥ The King's Egyptian Wife ✡

☥ **Amenhotep III**
He married his baby half-sister Sitamun (an Egyptian),

in order to inherit the throne, since the line of royal descent was through the eldest daughter.

✡ **Solomon**

The biblical Solomon ***"made affinity with Pharaoh king of Egypt, and took Pharaoh's daughter, and brought her into the city of David."*** (I Kings, 3:1)

☞ Points of interest in the biblical account:

1- The reference to Pharaoh's daughter as being Solomon's first and principal wife indicates, as in the case of Amenhotep III, that she was the wife of his own nationality. If Solomon was the king of Israel, he should have had an Israelite wife to bear his successor, since, according to Israelite tradition, the line of descent is from the mother. However, The Bible tells us that Solomon married only foreign wives.

2- The pharaoh whose daughter was married to Solomon was (as is the case, in the Bible, with all Egyptian pharaohs) never named. The pharaoh in question, however, is said to have ***"gone up, and taken Gezer, and burnt it with fire, and slain the Canaanites that dwelt in the city, and given it for a present unto his daughter, Solomon's wife"*** (I Kings, 9:16).

☞ This biblical verse has no historical validity.

None of the Egyptian kings, who lived during the supposed reign of Solomon, were involved in military campaigns in western Asia. The kings of this period belonged to the very weak Twenty-First Dynasty.

☥ The King and Foreign Wives ✡

☥ Amenhotep III loved foreign women. After marrying Sitamun to inherit the throne, he married Tiye, the daughter of Yuya (Joseph the Patriarch), an Israelite. Amenhotep III issued a scarab in celebration of his marriage to Tiye. Copies were sent to foreign princes, reading in part "**... the Great King's Wife, Tiye, who liveth. The name of her father is Yuya, the name of her mother is Tuya ...**"

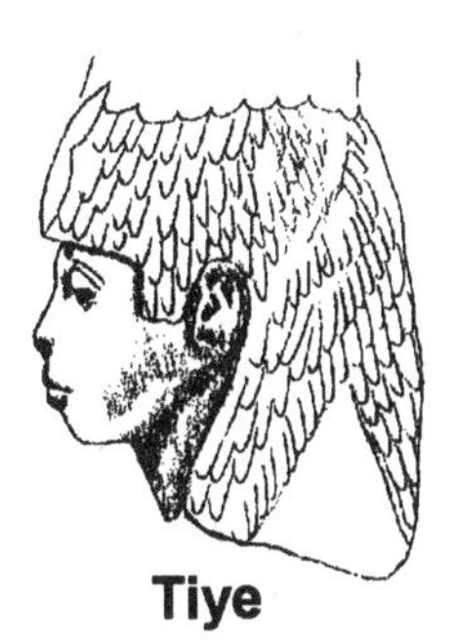

Tiye

He also married two women from Mitanni, two from Babylonia, as well as a princess from Arzawa, in south-western Asia Minor.

✡ Solomon is said to have had seven hundred wives and three hundred concubines (I Kings, 11:3). They were all foreigners: *"But King Solomon loved many strange women, together with the daughter of Pharaoh, women of the Moabites, Ammonites, Edomites, Zidonians and Hittites"* (I Kings, 11:1).

The Government

☥ **Amenhotep III Rule**

The administrative system attributed to the biblical Solomon does not belong to the Palestinian Israel, but to the period of the Egyptian Empire. The basis of such a governmental structure is a purely Egyptian system, which existed for more than 5,000 years.

✡ **Solomon Rule**

According to the Bible, Solomon did away with the tribal divisions, and united Israel together with other parts of the empire.

☞ **The bible would have us believe that the tribal society of the Hebrews, was integrated overnight into a sophisticated political system, under the control of the King and his central government. Furthermore, we are told that this political system vanished at the end of his forty-year reign, as abruptly and as mysteriously, as it began!**

☞ **There is no historical evidence of said political system to administer this vast empire, such as: taxation system, and an organized army to guard its boundaries.**

☞ **Almost all scholars agree that the taxation system, and the bureaucracy, which the Bible says was introduced by Solomon, match precisely the system that was used in Egypt at the time of Amenhotep III. (See *Historical Deception - The Untold Story of Ancient Egypt* for detailed comparison.)**

☥ The Great Builder ✡

☥ Amenhotep III was reputed to be a great builder. The construction activities at the sites mentioned below, in I Kings, 9:15, are very similar to the archaeological findings of work completed during the reign of Amenhotep III.

✡ Likewise, Solomon is reputed to have been a master

builder. He built *"the house of the Lord, and his own house, and Millo, and the wall of Jerusalem, and Hazer, and Megiddo, and Gezer"* (I Kings, 9:15) and numerous other building activities.

☞ No archaeological findings in the named building sites bore any inscription that identified a king named Solomon, or anything else related to his supposed kingdom.

☞ **To summarize, there is historical and archaeological evidence of building during the reign of Amenhotep III that matches those ascribed to Solomon. However, none of them are dated to the tenth century B.C., the supposed time when Solomon ruled. (See *Historical Deception - The Untold Story of Ancient Egypt* for the detailed analysis of the building activities mentioned in I Kings, 9:15.)**

☥ The Wisdom of The King ✡

☥ Amenhotep III was reputed to be a wise king.

✡ Solomon is described in the Bible as being very wise. *"King Solomon exceeded all the kings of the earth for riches and for wisdom"* (I Kings, 10:23).

The reasons given for such wisdom brings forth more similarities between Solomon and Amenhotep III.

Two areas will be discussed here:

1- The Bible attributes the authoring of the Books of Hebrew wisdom and poetry, to Solomon. It is hard to believe that the king was the composer of <u>all these books</u> of

Proverbs, of Ecclesiates and Wisdom, and of Psalms!

Where did all this wisdom literature come from? The answer is summarized in John Bright's finding: *"That parts of the Proverbs ... are based on the Egyptian Maxims of Amenemope (Amenhotep III) ... is well known".*

☞ Yet another confirmation that Solomon and Amenhotep III are one and the same person.

2- The most popular story about the wisdom of Solomon is his resolution of a dispute between two mothers, over the parenthood of a child, as mentioned in I Kings, 3:16-28. The story goes that two women, who lived in the same house, gave birth to baby boys. One baby died and both women claimed the surviving child as her own. They went before the king with their dispute. Solomon then ordered the child to be cut in half with a sword, so as to give one half to each woman. The real mother naturally tried to save the boy's life by letting the other woman have the boy. That is how Solomon identified the real mother.

☞ It is hard to believe that the king, who had professional judges and officials, would involve himself personally in such a dispute between two women who are described in the Bible as *"harlots"*. The king would not have personally sat in judgment of such a case, unless he had a personal interest.

☥ The biblical accounts in I Kings, 3:16-28 are strikingly similar to the Amenhotep III situation. The women involved were his wife, Queen Tiye, the mother of Moses (Akhenaton), and Tiy, Moses' nursing mother, who was already nursing Nefertiti, his sister. More details in the next chapter.

☥ The King and Foreign Gods ✡

☥ Amenhotep III was diverted and converted to the worship of the Aton, the God who became identified with the Hebrew Jehovah (the Lord), as Adonai. He is shown in a stele (now at the British Musuem) being given the key of life by the rays of the sun disc of Aton. He also continued his belief in the other Egyptian neteroo (gods).

✡ The Bible tells us that Solomon was diverted to other gods: *"King Solomon loved many strange women, together with the daughter of Pharaoh, women of the Moabites, Ammonites, Edomites, Zidonians, and Hittites; Of the nations concerning which the Lord said unto the children of Israel, Ye shall not go in to them, neither shall they come in unto you; for surely they will turn away your heart after their gods: Solomon clave unto these in love"* (I Kings, 11:1-2).

"For it came to pass, when Solomon was old, that his wives turned away his heart after other gods: and his heart was not perfect with the Lord his God, as was the heart of David his father." (I Kings, 11:4).

☥ Different Eras ☥

Despite the hard work of biblical scholars, historians and archaeologists, no single piece of evidence has been found to support the period of the supposed United Monarchy of David and Solomon. Scholars have been confused by the biblical chronology, which present David and Solomon as having belonged to the period following both the Exodus and the settlement in the "Promised Land".

Many of these biblical events occurred four to five centuries earlier than what the Old Testament would have us believe. Both Tuthomosis III, the historical King David, and his great-grandson Amenhotep III, the Biblical Solomon, belonged to the Eighteenth Dynasty of Egypt.

The biblical scribes were so bold as to manipulate historical events. They wrote their accounts in a historical fashion, but there is no historical evidence to support their manipulated accounts.

19

The Tyrant Father

Akhenaton *(Moses)*

General

☥ Akhenaton has been called by many *the first monotheist.* He glorified one Egyptian neter (god), namely *Aton*, over and above all the other neteroo (gods). His actions were intended to challenge the establishment of the neter (god) Amen, at Thebes. His vendetta with Amen was motivated as much by politics as by religion, as will be detailed later in this chapter.

✡ Likewise, the God of Moses declared '*... against all the gods of Egypt I will execute judgement; I am the Lord.*' (Exodus, 12:12)

Akhenaton shut down the temples of the other neteroo (gods) of Egypt, cut off financial support for them and sent the priests home.

Throughout Egypt, he ordered the name of Amen, the supreme deity of Thebes, to be erased from the inscriptions of the temples. Akhenaton's reign extended eighteen years, much of it as co-regent. After he abdicated the throne, the worship of Amen was reinstated. The works of Akhenaton were destroyed. His name was deleted throughout the rest of Egyptian history. He was referred to as *the criminal*, *the rebel* and *mos* which means *rightful person/heir*.

In order to judge his behavior, one must ask the people of any country what their reaction would be if their leader decided that his church, of all the churches, was the only right one. Would they call him an enlightened monotheist? Furthermore, what if this leader decided to actually close all other churches, because, in his view, they were no good? Would he be called an enlightened monotheist?

The people of any country would surely react as ancient Egyptians reacted, because their leader would not be an enlightened monotheist, but a tyrannical dictator.

☥ Sigmund Freud Research ✡

- Sigmund Freud, the Jewish father of psychoanalysis, was interested in reading about Akhenaton and Moses. He later wrote a book called Moses and Monotheism. Sigmund Freud argued that Moses was an Egyptian, a follower of Akhenaton, who later led the Jews out of Egypt.

- Freud also came to the conclusion that *Moses* was itself an Egyptian name.

Even though the Bible in Exodus, 2:10 tells us that Moses' royal mother, who adopted him, called him **Moshe** because, she said, ***"I drew him out of the water"***, Freud demonstrated that *Moshe* had a different meaning. In fact, the name **Moshui**, is the Hebrew name which means *one who has been drawn out.* It was then Freud's conclusion that the name of the Jewish leader was not of Hebrew origin, but rather from an Egyptian origin.

• Later, Freud came very close to demonstrating that Akhenaton and Moses were one and the same person. In 1937 Imago published another article by Freud under the title **'If Moses was an Egyptian'**. Freud found great similarity between the new religion that Akhenaton had tried to impose on his country and the religious teaching ascribed to Moses. Sigmund Freud wrote: *"The Jewish creed says: 'Schema Yisrael Adonai Elohenu Adonai Echod'."* ('Hear, 0 Israel, the Lord thy God is one God'.) The Hebrew letter *d* is equivalent to the Egyptian letter *t*. Therefore this sentence from the Jewish creed could be translated: *"Hear, 0 Israel, our God Aton is the only God."* This is a mirror image of Akhenaton's creed which has also declared that Aton is the only God.

Childhood

☥ Akhenaton's father, Amenhotep III, met and fell in love with Tiye, the daughter of Yuya (identified in the Bible as the Israelite Joseph the Patriarch). In order to inherit the throne, however, Amenhotep III married his half-sister Sitamun. He shortly thereafter married Tiye, the half-Egyptian/half-Israelite. To add insult to injury, he made Tiye rather than Sitamun, his Great Royal Wife (queen).

Tiye

Amenhotep III's marital actions were irresponsible and must have created a poisonous atmosphere.

Later, Tiye had a son, Tuthomosis, who was educated and trained at Memphis and who held the title of the High Priest of Ptah, as did most heirs-apparent during the Eighteenth Dynasty. But then he disappeared suddenly from the scene. There may have been an imminent danger awaiting Tiye's sons. She was of mixed Egyptian-Israelite blood, and if her son succeeded to the throne, this would be regarded as forming a new dynasty of non-Egyptian, part-Israelite rulers over Egypt.

Her second son was born, probably in 1394 B.C., at the fortified frontier city of Zarw. He was named Amenhotep IV (later to be known as Akhenaton).

☥ Upon Akhenaton's birth, Tiye sent him by water to the safety of her Israelite relations at nearby Goshen.

✡ This event is echoed in the biblical story of Moses being found by a princess in the bulrushes by the bank of the Nile.

✡ The imminent danger to Tiye's sons is echoed in the Talmud which provides a different reason for the attempt to kill Moses at birth. It was Moses specifically (not all other Hebrew children) who was to be murdered because he posed a threat to the throne of Egypt.

✡ The Bible gave the impression that Moses was the first-born in his family. We find out later that he already had an elder sister, Miriam, who was watching him floating on the water. She approached the pharaoh's daughter and offered: ***"Shall I fetch one of the Hebrew women to nurse the baby for you?"*** When the offer was accepted, the sister got her mother. The mother agreed to nurse her own baby in return for payment.

Later, when the child grew older, she took him back to the pharaoh's daughter, who adopted him as her son. Then she, we are told, gave him the name *Moshe*.

☞ Some comments about these biblical events:

☞ **1-** When an earlier pharaoh appointed the Patriarch Joseph as his vizier, he gave him an Egyptian name to go with his new Egyptian identity. Does it make sense for the Egyptian royal mother of Moses to give her adopted Egyptian son a Hebrew name?!

☞ **2-** Can we expect the Egyptian royal mother to have sufficient, or any, knowledge of the Hebrew language to be able to choose a special Hebrew name for the child?

☞ **3-** The biblical claim that the pharaoh's daughter adopted the child is inherently improbable. The customs of the time would not have allowed an unmarried princess to adopt a child.

☞ **4-** Finally, the biblical story of two mothers fighting over the parenthood of a child who went to Solomon to resolve their dispute (I Kings 3:16-28) is strikingly similar to the account of Moses growing up in the pharaoh's palace, where he had "two mothers". Solomon, the King of Kings, would not have gotten involved in a dispute between two women, unless the dispute was in his household.

Youth

☥ Akhenaton, spent most of his youth in the Eastern Delta and at Heliopolis. In the Eastern Delta area he was influenced by Aton, a God without an image. At Heliopolis, he was educated by the priests of Ra, the ancient Egyptian solar deity.

✡ Likewise, early historians stated that the biblical Moses spent his early youth at Heliopolis.

• • •

☥ When he was in his very early teens, Amenhotep IV was finally allowed to take up residence at Thebes. The Amenite priests and nobles of Egypt, the protectors of old traditions, regarded Akhenaton with contempt for his mixed race. It was not he who first rejected them, it was they, the Amenists, who refused to accept him as the legitimate heir to the throne.

The Queen Mother

• When Akhenaton's father, namely Amenhotep III's health began to deteriorate, Tiye's power increased correspondingly. In order to ensure her son's inheritance of the throne, she arranged for him to marry his half-sister, Nefertiti, who was the daughter of Amenhotep III by Sitamun, the legitimate heiress. It is Nefertiti who is recognized in the Bible as Miriam, Moses' sister.

• Tiye prompted her husband, Amenhotep III, to appoint Amenhotep IV (Akhenaton) as his co-regent.

• Queen Tiye was definitely the power behind the throne, at the time. Her name, unlike that of earlier queens, was placed regularly in a cartouche, a distinction previously limited to the ruling monarch.

The Name "Moses"

☥ In the name Moses, the *s* at the end of the name is drawn from the Greek translation of the biblical name. Without the last letter *s*, the name is Mose.

As mentioned earlier, in both Hebrew and Egyptian, short vowels, although always pronounced, were never written. If we take away the two vowels, *o* and *e* from the name, we are left with only two consonants *m* and *s*. *MS* is commonly pronounced as *Mos*.

Mos was part of many compound Egyptian names such as *Ptah-mos* and *Tuth-mos*. We also find some examples of the word *mos* being used on its own as a personal pronoun and which means *rightful person*. Such practice began during the Eighteenth Dynasty.

✡ If we take away the two vowels *o* and *e* from Moshe (the Jewish name for Moses) we are left with only two consonants, *m* and *sh*.

☞ As the Hebrew letter *sh* is the equivalent of the Egyptian *s*, one is able to conclude that the Hebrew word *Moshe* and the Egyptian word *Mos* are one and the same.

✡ As explained earlier, the biblical explanation of the name Moses is incorrect. The Israelites may have called him ***mos*** to indicate that he was the legitimate son of Amenhotep III and the rightful heir to his father's throne.

✡ Many generations later and in a different country, the biblical editor, who may not have had any knowledge of Moses' original name, attempted to provide a Hebrew explanation of the name. It is also possible that the biblical editor was trying to remove any possible link between Moses and his position as the Pharaoh of Egypt.

☥ Aton Worship ✡

☥ There were very many neteroo (gods) in Egypt. Some deities had only local distinction. Others, like Amen, Ra and Osiris, were recognized throughout Egypt. Aton was among this multitude of deities, and it was not a new idea which was introduced by Akhenaton. Aton does appear in a few texts from the time of the Twelfth Dynasty. It appeared frequently since the time of Tuthomosis IV (1401-1391 B.C.). Akhenaton exalted Aton over and above the others. Aton is the disk of the sun as physical manifestation of Ra. Aton had no image, unlike the other neteroo (gods).

✡ The Lord of the Jews, who like Aton, had no image, is called *Adon* (Adonai means *my Lord*).

☞ Since both Akhenaton and Moses worshipped the same Aton/Adon, this is further proof that they are one and the same.

• • •

☞ The hymn to Aton which is attributed to Akhenaton is a mirror image of Psalm 104. Below, are both versions for you to compare:

☥ **Hymn to the Aton**

The cattle are content in their pasture, the trees and plants are green, the birds fly from their nests. Their wings are raised in praise of your soul. The goats leap on their feet. All flying and fluttering things live when you shine for them. Likewise the boats race up and down the river, and every way is open, because you have appeared. The fish in the river leap before your face. Your rays go to the depth of the sea.

✡ **Psalm 104**

He causeth the grass to grow for the cattle, and the herb for the service of man: that he may bring forth food out of the earth: and wine that maketh glad the heart of man and oil to make his face shine, and bread which strengtheneth man's heart. The trees of the Lord are full of sap: the cedars of Lebanon which he hath planted: where the birds make their nests: as for the stork, the fir trees are her house. The high hills are a refuge for the wild goats; and the rocks for the conies.... So is this great and wide sea, wherein are things creeping innumerable, both great and small beasts. There go the ships.

☞ The similarity of sequence and of images in both compositions is too striking to be a coincidence. As such, many believe that the earlier Egyptian hymn must have been known to the later Hebrew writer.

• • •

☥ Akhenaton chose the Heliopolitan solar form of the Egyptian temple, to be used as the place for the worship of the Aton.

✡ Likewise, Moses was the first person to introduce a temple into Israelite worship, when he created the tabernacle in Sinai.

• • •

☥ Akhenaton adopted the Egyptian practice of a holy boat, which was usually kept in the temple. The ark was used to carry the deity during processions.

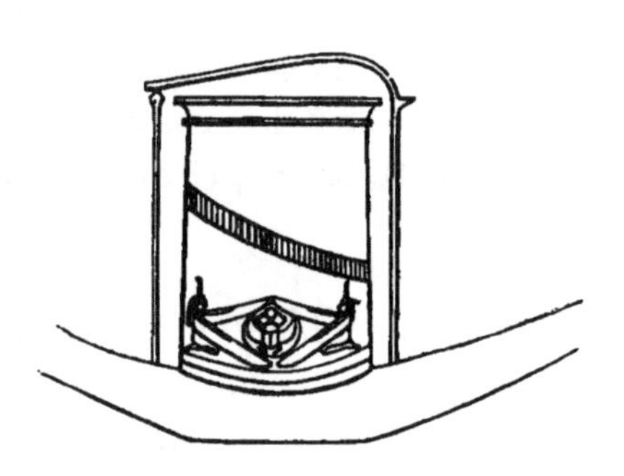

✡ Moses also introduced the ark, where the Pentateuch scrolls were kept (Exodus, 25:10). The ark is respected as the second holiest part of the Jewish temple, after the Pentateuch itself.

☥ Akhenaton adopted the Egyptian priesthood system and associated rituals.

✡ There was no Israelite priesthood before the time of Moses. Rituals and worship of the newly-established Israelite priesthood were similar to those introduced by Akhenaton. Moses arranged the priesthood in two main levels, the high priest and the ordinary priests. Instructions were issued to them about their specific garment, purification, annointment and how to go about fulfilling the duties of their offices.

• • •

☥ Across the Nile from Tell-el Amarna, there is the city of Mal-lawi (Mal-Levi), which means literally *The City of the Levites*. The Levites held priestly positions with Akhenaton at Amarna.

✡ Likewise, the Levites held priestly positions with Moses, according to the Bible.

• • •

☥ Akhenaton's two highest priestly officials were:

1- **Meryre II** who was the High Priest of the Aton, at the Amarna temple.

2- **Panehesy** who was the Chief Servitor of the Aton at Akhenaton's temple.

✡ Likewise, Moses' two highest priestly officials were:

1- ***Merari***, who is described in Genesis, 46:11 as one of the sons of Levi. The Egyptian equivalent of his name is *Meryre*.

2- *Phinehas*, who was the son of Eleazar and grandson of Aaron according to Exodus, 6:25. His name in the Talmud is Pinhas. The Egyptian equivalent of his name is *Panehesy*.

☞ **It is therefore evident that we are dealing with the same high officials who served Akhenaton at Amarna and then accompanied him to Sinai afterwards. Yet another confirmation that Moses and Akhenaton are one and the same.**

☥ The Ruler ☥

Akhenaton's eighteen-year reign was mostly a co-regency. He reigned the first twelve years in conjunction with his father, Amenhotep III. It was very probable that the last few years of his reign was a co-regency with his brother Semenkhkare.

1- Early Co-Regency Rule

Akhenaton became a co-regent in or about Year 28 of Amenhotep III. About Year 33, he transferred his residence to his new capital city, Tell el-Amarna, 200 miles north of Thebes. His reign had two groups of dated inscriptions. One related to the Thebes residence, which started at Year 28 of Amenhotep III. The other one was related to the Amarna residence. A correspondence in date, year by year, between the two groups of inscriptions can be easily established. For example, Year 28 of Amenhotep III equals Year 1 of Amenhotep IV. Year 33 of Amenhotep III is equal to Year 6 of Amenhotep IV, ...etc. Amenhotep III died in his Year 38, which was Akhenaton's Year 12.

From the start of the co-regency, Amenhotep IV offended

the Amenite priesthood by building temples to his God, the Aton, within the boundaries of the established Amen-Ra temples at Karnak. He also did not invite the traditional priests to any of the festivities. In his fifth year he changed his name to Akhenaton in honor of the Aton.

Because of the hostile climate which he created, Akhenaton, and his father, Amenhotep III, left Thebes and went to their new capital city at Tell el-Amarna (two hundred miles north of Thebes). Amenhotep named his new city Akhetaton meaning *the city of the horizon of the Aton.* The co-regency ended when his father died in Akhenaton's Year 12.

- The issue of the co-regency between Amenhotep III and his son, Akhenaton, was further reinforced by the discovery of his vizier's tomb in late 1989, namely Aper-el. The main points to be drawn from these findings are:

1- Akhenaton could only have had a vizier, if he was ruling.

2- Since Amenhotep III was mentioned, in the vizier's tomb, by his praenomen, Neb-Maat-Re, and in accordance with Egyptian traditions, it must be concluded that Amenhotep III was still alive when Akhenaton was in charge.

3- The fact that Akhenaton's vizier was a worshipper of El (short for Elohim) confirms the strong bond between the king and the Israelites living in Egypt at the time. Such a bond is also evident in the many found pieces of funerary items. They included a box given to Aper-el by Amenhotep III and Queen Tiye, as well as Amenhotep III's cartouche.

2- Sole Ruler

• When Akhenaton became sole ruler after Amenhotep III died, Year 12 of Akhenaton, he shut down the other temples, stopped all financial support for them and sent the priests home. These actions made a bad situation worse. Throughout his reign, Akhenaton relied completely on the army's support for protection. This military climate is depicted in the tombs of the nobles, at Tell-el Amarna.

3- Late Co-Regency Rule

• As a last resort or as a ploy, Akhenaton, in his Year 15, was forced to install his brother, Semenkhkare, as his co-regent at Thebes. This action only delayed the inevitable outcome.

Semenkhare, who was used and victimized by his own brother

• As a sign of trouble between Akhenaton and Nefertiti, her official name Neferneferuaten, meaning *beloved of Akhenaton*, was given to Semenkhkare, upon his accession to the throne.

• Semenkhkare left Amarna for Thebes, where he reversed Akhenaton's hostile actions and began building a temple to Amen.

• In his Year 17, Akhenaton suddenly disappeared. At or about the same time, Semenkhkare died suddenly. The co-regency of Akhenaton and Semenkhkare was succeeded by the young prince, Tut-Ankh-Amen.

• In his Year 17, Akhenaton may have been warned by his uncle, Aye, of a threat on his life. He abdicated and fled to

Sinai, with a small group of followers, taking with him his symbol of pharaonic authority, a staff topped by a brass serpent (similar to the "magic" rod of Moses).

Although Sinai was part of Egypt from the early days of Egyptian history, there was no established governing authority there. It was more or less a buffer zone between Egypt and its eastern neighbors.

✡ The sudden disappearance of Akhenaton is echoed in the biblical story of Moses when he escaped to Sinai, after he slew an Egyptian. The account of how Moses slew an Egyptian may have been mentioned in the Amarna Tablets. Among them is a letter, sent from Abd-Khiba, King of Jerusalem, to Akhenaton, in which Abd-Khiba accuses Akhenaton of not punishing some Hebrews who killed two Egyptian officials: "... **the Khabiru (Hebrews) are seizing the towns of the king ... Turbazu has been slain in the very gate of Zilu (Zarw), yet the king holds back ... Yaptih-Hadad has been slain in the very gate of Zilu, yet the king holds back.**"

☞ **Was letting the Israelites get away with two murders, the final blow to Akhenaton's reign?**

4- King Without Power

Even though Akhenaton abdicated and fled from the scene, he was still regarded as the legitimate ruler. As long as he was alive, the pharaoh was regarded as being the lawful ruler of his lands, even if he was weak and had no authority.

When the ten-year-old Tut-Ankh-Aton became the official pharaoh, he was assigned and controlled by a guardian. This would be similar to any monarchy nowadays when the legal heir is a minor. As such, the rule of Akhenaton, his father, continued for four years, and during this time the boy King was still called Tut-Ankh-**Aton**.

Four years later, Year 21 of Akhenaton, the young King abandoned the Aton (at least officially) and became the son of Amen. Simultaneously, he changed his name from Tut-Ankh-**Aton** to Tut-Ankh-**Amen**. The Amen priesthood accepted this new allegance in a crowning celebration. Only then did he become the legitimate monarch.

At this point in time, the Aton lost its power in Egypt, and Akhenaton, who was still alive in Sinai, was king no more.

☥ Nefertiti The Beloved ☥

☥ Queen Nefertiti is described in the tomb of one of the officials of Akhenaton as the one who **"unites her beauties and propitiates the Aton with her pleasant voice and with her beautiful hands holding the sistra"**. Nefertiti means **'the beautiful one has come'**.

☥ When Semenkhkare became co-regent, Nefertiti disappeared mysteriously and some scholars suggested, without any evidence, that she must have died around that time. There is evidence that she moved to the north City of Amarna where Tut-Ankh-Amen was also resident. Objects inscribed with the queen's name have been found at the residence in the city of Amarna. One can deduce that she may have disagreed with her husband, and that her views proved to be right after all. There is no evidence that she was later buried in her royal tomb.

☥ When Akhenaton abolished the worship of Isis among other deities, Nefertiti's image was used in place of that of the mother netert (goddess) on Amarna funerary objects. Nefertiti's image was later found, in place of the image of Isis in the empty and broken sarcophagus of Akhenaton.

Akhenaton's Capital City Akhetaton (Amarna)

☥ Contrary to the general view, the name Amarna was not derived from a Moslem Arab tribe which settled in the area. No evidence exists to substantiate such a claim. The name is, however, derived from the name in the second cartouche of Akhenaton's god, namely *Im-r-n*.

✡ Amram, or Imran, was the name given in the Bible to Moses' father, and it is precisely the same name Akhenaten gave to his *father*, the Aton.

☞ Yet another confirmation that Moses and Akhenaton are one and the same.

• • •

☥ The house of the high priest **Panehesy** was located prominently in the city. He was never buried in his assigned tomb.

✡ Panehesy is equated to the biblical *Phinehas/Pinhas*, the priest, who according to the Talmud, killed Jesus.

Amarna Letters

The Amarna letters were discovered in 1887. They consist of a collection of several hundred clay tablets written in Babylonian cuneiform. The letters were sent to Akhenaton and Amenhotep III from other kings and rulers of the adjoining lands. Egypt's replies to these letters were destroyed, so we have only one side of the correspondence. By inference however, it is quite possible to guess many subject matters of concern.

The Aftermath

• Semenkhkare died suddenly and mysteriously at Thebes. It was impossible to give him a proper burial with so much turmoil in the country. Semenkhkare was therefore buried secretly, and in a hurry, using some objects meant to be used by Akhenaton, who had already fled from Amarna to Sinai.
Incidentally some of Semenkhkare's funerary equipment at Amarna, was later used for Tut-Ankh-Amen who also died suddenly. Semenkhkare was succeeded in his turn by the young king Tut-Ankh-Aton, the son of Akhenaton (Moses).

• Tut-Ankh-Amen ruled for at least nine, and perhaps ten years (c. 1361-1352 B.C.) before meeting an early death.

• Tut was succeeded by Aye (Ephraim), his great-uncle and the last of the four Amarna kings.
Aye ruled for only four years before he disappeared. Nothing much is known about his death. His mummy — if he was ever mummified — was never found. His tomb, in the Valley of the Kings, was usurped by his successor, Horemheb (known in the Bible as the ***Pharaoh of Oppression***).

The Exile (Talmudic Ethiopia/Egyptian Amarna)

✡ According to the Talmud, when Moses was 18, he fled Egypt, after killing an Egyptian. He then became a soldier and fought on the side of the King of Ethiopia, against a rebellion led by an Egyptian native, Bi'lam. After the King won, Moses became very popular. As a result, when the king died, Moses was appointed as their new king and ***"they gave him the widow of their king for a wife."***

Moses reigned ***'in justice and righteousness'***. But the Queen of Ethiopia, Adonith, wanted her own son by the dead king to rule. She said to the people: ***"Why should this stranger continue to rule over you?"*** The Talmud account goes, that even though the people loved and wanted him, Moses resigned voluntarily, and departed from their land. The people of Ethiopia bestowed great honors upon him.

☞ There are many similarities between The Talmud story of Moses and the Akhenaton story at Amarna:

1- Moses was elevated to the post of king for some time before going to Sinai. Akhenaton likewise.

2- Moses officiated as the high priest. Akhenaton likewise.

3- The name of the Egyptian queen who became the wife of Moses is given as Adonith (Aton-it). Her name is clearly derived from the Aton, who was Akhenaton's god.

4- The queen's desire to place her son on the throne instead of Moses, is similar to Queen Nefertiti's desire to place her son, Tut-Ankh-Amen, on the throne instead of his father, Akhenaton.

5- The Talmud reference to Ethiopia, which is described as being a city, was mistaken for the Amarna location.

The Tomb of Akhenaton

No evidence has ever been found regarding the date of Akhenaton's death. The account of the reign of Moses in the Talmud, as a King of Nubia (Ethiopia), indicates that he resigned his post, but did not die at that time.

See *Historical Deception - The Untold Story of Ancient Egypt* for the details of the supporting evidence regarding Akhenaton's death, as well as:

- probable reasons for the manipulation of historical events in the Bible.

- more information on the Jewish sojourn in Egypt, the Exodus, the death of Moses/Akhenaton and the so-called Israel Stele.

Epilogue

20

The Egyptian/Christian Similarities

Previous chapters identified some biblical characters as historical Egyptian figures. The following are a few other similarities, as they relate to theological practices, between the Bible and ancient Egypt.

1- Egyptologist Sir E. A. Wallis Budge wrote, *"The new religion (Christianity) which was preached there by St. Mark and his immediate followers, in all essentials so closely resembled that which was the outcome of the worship of Osiris, Isis, and Horus that popular opposition was entirely disarmed."*

   The similarities, noted by Budge and everyone who has compared the Egyptian Osiris/Isis/Horus legend to the Gospel story, are powerful. Both accounts are practically the same, e.g. the supernatural conception, the divine birth, the struggles against the enemy in the wilderness, and the resurrection from the dead to eternal life. The main difference between them, is that the Gospel tale is considered historical and the Isis/Osiris/Horus cycle is a myth. The spiritual message of the Osiris/Isis/Horus myth and the Christian revelation is exactly the same.

2- Gerald Massey, after studying the similarities between the Osiris/Isis/Horus myth and the Gospel story, concluded in his book *Ancient Egypt*, 1970, that the Christian revelation is Egyptian in source. He believed that early Christians in their 'ignorance' (his word) took the Egyptian spiritual teaching and turned it into a spiritual and historical event.

3- Many elements of the Isis myth and the story of the Virgin Mary are very similar, for both were able to conceive without the male impregnation. Horus was conceived and born after the death of Isis' husband, and as such, she was revered as the Virgin Mother.

The Virgin and Her Son

Isis is the divine power responsible for the creation of all living creatures.

4- According to ancient legend, any woman who truly loves her husband is Isis, and has the power of awakening him into greater life as Horus. Father S.J. Vann draws a similar comparison to the awakening of Christ by Mary Magdalene as Christ emerges from the tomb.

5- An ancient Egyptian festival celebrating the birth of Horus, was held towards the end of the Egyptian year, and it resembles the Christian festival of Christmas.

The celebration was called "**the Day of the Child in his Cradle**" and was held at the court and the chapel of the Dendara Temple.

6- The spheres of angels and archangels in Christianity are strikingly similar to ancient Egypt's heirachy of Neteroo *(gods)*.

We talked earlier about the Egyptian neteroo (gods) as the personifications of universal principles, functions and attributes of the One great and supreme God.

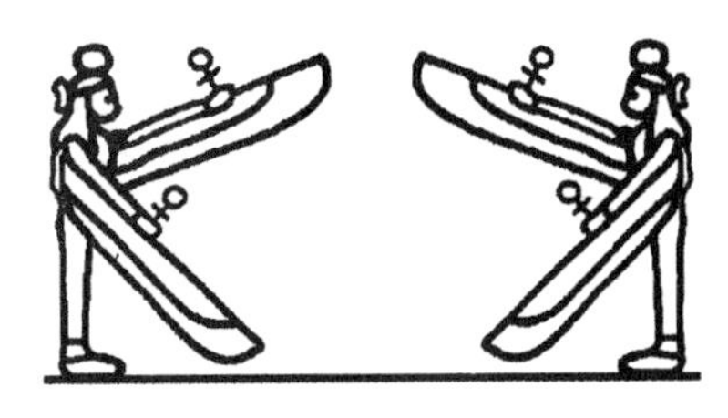

The Song of Moses in Deuteronomy (32:43), as found in a cave at Qumran near the Dead Sea, mentions the word *gods* in the plural: ***"Rejoice, O heavens, with him; and do obeisance to him, ye gods."*** When the passage is quoted in the New Testament (Hebrews, 1:6), the word *gods* is substituted with *angels of God*. As such, The neteroo who were called *gods* by some, were endorsed and incorporated into Christianity under a new name, *angels*.

7- Daily life activities are portrayed, on the walls of the ancient Egyptian tombs, in the presence of the neteroo (gods) or with the assistance of the neteroo (gods). The typical Egyptian sowing and reaping scene is symbolically similar to the Bible's ***"Whatsoever a man soweth, that shall he also reap."***

8- The walls of the ancient Egyptian tombs show vintners pressing new wine. The process of wine making is a metaphor for spiritual processes. Such is the case also in the biblical wine symbolism.

9- A recurrent theme, on the walls of many Egyptian tombs, is the relief of a woman shown sniffing at the lotus. The lotus played a complex and significant role in the symbolism ofEgypt. The perfume of the lotus is its spiritualized essence, similar to the ***odor of sanctity*** in Christian doctrine.

10- Various fishing nets and traps are portrayed on the walls of the ancient Egyptian tombs. In other texts, Horus becomes a fisherman and his four sons also fish for him. This is another parallel between Christian and Egyptian symbolism. Christ used the symbolism several times and

he made his disciples fishers of men.

11- The most distinctive Egyptian symbol is the eye, which plays many complex and subtle roles. The eye is called the Eye of Ra, symbolizing the sun.

The physical eye is to man what the sun is to Ra. The eye is the part of the body able to perceive the light, and is therefore a symbol for the spiritual ability.

One of the texts, in the Egyptian Book of the Caverns, describes the unilluminated: "*They are like this, those who do not see the Great God, who do not perceive the rays of his disk, whose souls do not leave the earth, who do not hear the words of this Great God when he passes near to their cavern.*" The description is very similar to the Gospel references to those with ***"eyes to see and ears to hear."***

12- Dancing at the temples was common for both Egyptians and biblical characters.

- In the Hall of Offerings, at Dendara Temple, a song celebrating the taming of the lioness, goes:

The King of Egypt, Pharaoh comes to dance
He comes to sing.
You, his Lady, see how he dances,
Wife of Horus
See how he springs.

✞ Similarly, Christ is celebrated as *"Lord of the Dance"* in a Christmas carol from the Middle Ages.

✡ The Biblical David himself danced before the ark (I Chron, 15:29).

✡ The Jews considered it part of their religious duties to approach the Deity with the dance, with the timbrel, and with the harp (Exodus, 15:20).

The King sings and dances in the temple

✡ The mode by which the Jews worshipped the golden calf consisted of songs and dancing; which was immediately derived from the ceremonies of the Egyptians.

13- The Egyptian word for paper was **Pa-pe-ra**. The Greeks called it *papyrus*. One can easily see that the English word, *paper,* came from the Egyptian **pa-pe-ra**.

Your dictionary will also confirm that the word ***Bible*** is of an Egyptian origin. The *Bible*, or book, was derived from ***byblos***, which is the Egyptian hieratic word for papyrus.

14- There are many Egyptian texts which have notable parallels in the Bible, and outstanding among them is the hymn composed in honor of the Aton by Akhenaton, and Psalm 104. They are both amazingly similar in all particulars, sequence and images. (Read both under the chapter, *The Tyrant Father*.)

15- The theme in the Egyptian Book of the Caverns talks about the necessity for death and dissolution (of the carnal and material), prior to the birth of the spiritual. This is echoed by Christ when he says, ***"Except a corn of wheat fall into the ground and die, it abideth alone: but if it die, it bringeth forth much fruit"*** (John 12:24). Paul also refers to the same principle in I Corinthians 15:36, ***". . . that which thou sowest is not quickened, except it die."***

16- A text from the Egyptian Book of Night reads:

To come out of the Netherworld, to rest in the Morning Barge, to navigate the Abyss until the hour of Re, She who sees the beauty of her Lord, to make transformations in Khepri, to rise to the horizon, to enter the mouth, to come out of the vulva, to burst forth out of the Gate of the Horizon of the Hour, She who lifts up the beauty of Ra in order to make live men, all cattle, all worms he has created.

The description is very similar to Genesis 1:24, where God says, ***"Let the earth bring forth the living creature after his kind, cattle, and creeping thing ..."***

17- The thirty chapters of the Teaching of Amenemope (Amenhotep III) contain many wisdom texts which were later adopted in the Old Testament's Book of Proverbs. Numerous verbal parallels occur between this Egyptian text and the Bible, such as the opening lines of the first chapter: **"Give your ears, listen to the words which are spoken, give your mind to interpreting them. It is profitable to put them in your heart".**

18- The Egyptian cosmology was divided into four separate but complementary teachings, each with its center of worship. These teachings are strikingly similar to the detailed versions of the various stages outlined in the opening chapter of Genesis.

19- St, John's Gospel begins, ***"In the beginning was the Word, and the Word was with God, and the Word was God."*** The Egyptian *Book of the Coming Forth by Day* (commonly known as the *Book of the Dead*), the oldest written text in the world, contains a strikingly parallel passage, "**I am the Eternal, I am Ra ... I am that which created the Word ... I am the Word ...**"

20- In the ancient Egyptian teachings the spirit of the deceased, at the Judgment Day, denies committing each sin/fault before its assigned judge, by reciting the forty-two negative confessions (analogous to the famed **Ten Commandments**). These negative confessions come from *The Book of the Coming Forth by Day* (wrongly known as *The Book of the Dead*).

The Forty-two Judges

21- In the three religions of Judaism, Christianity and Islam, whenever the faithful pray, regardless of language, they always end their prayer by saying **Amen**. There is no linguistic translation for Amen, because it is a name and not a word. The origin of Amen is Egyptian, for Amen was the name of God. The Jews have learned about Amen during their sojourn in Egypt, which lasted for four generations.

The name of Amen, which means *the Hidden One*, in ancient Egypt, lives on.

22- Mut is the companion of Amen at Thebes. Mut is usually depicted as a woman wearing a vulture headdress, sometimes she is shown with the body of the vulture so artfully forming her own head that it passes for a headdress. The choice of the vulture for this particular feminine role is possibly because:

1- The vulture is supposed to be particularly zealous in caring for its young.

2- Legends were told that the vulture had no male species. The female vulture impregnated herself by exposing herself to the winds (i.e. gods). The vulture is therefore a symbol of virgin birth.

23- Khnum, in Egyptian, means **"molder"**. Khnum is usually shown as a ram-headed deity working at his potter's wheel, fashioning men and all living creatures out of clay.

A passage from an Egyptian creation legend by Khnum follows:

> **The mud of the Nile, heated to excess by the Sun, fermented and generated, without seeds, the races of men and animals.**

Passages of the Bible leave no doubt about the belief in the concept of the Divine Potter. Genesis, 2:7 mentions the material used to make man, the same type of substance used by Khnum:

"And the Lord God formed man of the dust of the ground, and breathed into his nostrils the breath of life; and man became a living soul."

The well-known ancient Egyptian illustration showing Khnum, the Divine Potter, at his potter's wheel, fashioning men from clay, was echoed thousands of years later in Isaiah, 64:8:

"Yet, O Lord, thou art our Father; we are the clay, and thou art our potter; we are all the work of thy hand."

AMEN

BIBLIOGRAPHY

Budge, Sir E.A. Wallis. *Egyptian Language, Easy Lessons in Egyptian Hieroglyphics*. New York, 1983.

Carter, Howard and A.C. Mace. *The Discovery of the Tomb of Tutankhamen*. New York, 1977.

Carter, Howard. *The Tomb of Tutankhamen*. Cassell, London, 1933.

Conder, C.R. *The Tell Amarna Tablets*. London, 1893.

Edwards, I.E.S. *Tutankhamun's Jewelry*. New York, 1976.

Erman, Adolf. *Life in Ancient Egypt*. New York, 1971.

Freud, Sigmund. *Moses and Monotheism*. London, 1951.

Gadalla, Moustafa. *Historical Deception, The Untold Story of Ancient Egypt*. Erie, PA, U.S.A., 1996.

Gardiner, Alan. *Egypt of the Pharaohs*. Oxford, 1961.

James, T.G.H. *An Introduction to Ancient Egypt*. London, 1979.

Josephus, Flavius. *Against Apion*, tr. H. St J. Thackeray. London, 1926.

Kenyon, Kathleen M. *The Bible and Recent Archaeology*, rev. ed. by P.R.S. Moorey. London, 1987.

Lambelet, K. *How to Read Hieroglyphics*. Cairo, 1974.

Massey, Gerald. *Ancient Egypt*. New York, 1970.

Neubert, Otto. *Tutankhamun and the Valley of the Kings*. New York, 1977.

Osman, Ahmed. *The House of the Messiah*. London, 1994.

Osman, Ahmed. *Moses, Pharaoh of Egypt*. London, 1991.

Osman, Ahmed. *Stranger in the Valley of the Kings*. London, 1989.

Polano, H. *Selections from the Talmud*. London, 1894

Wagner, N.E. *Abraham and David*. Toronto, 1972.

Wagner, N.E. *Studies on the Ancient Palestinian World*. Toronto, 1972.

West, John A. *Serpent in the Sky - The High Wisdom of Ancient Egypt*. Wheaton, IL, 1993.

West, John A. *The Travelers Key to Ancient Egypt*. New York, 1989.

Wilkinson, Sir J. Gardner. *The Ancient Egyptians, Their Life and Customs*. London, 1988.

Yadin, Yigael. *Hazor*. London, 1975.

————. *The Egyptian Book of the Dead*. New York, 1967.

————. *Jewish Encyclopedia*, managing editor Isidore Singer. New York and London, 1904.

INDEX

A

B

C

D

E

F

N

O

P

R

S

T

W

Y

Z

About Bastet Publishing

Bastet Publishing specializes in publishing reader-friendly books about ancient Egyptian history, daily activities, achievements, and their ever-lasting influence on the world, past and present. Our books are engaging, factual, well researched, practical, interesting and appealing to the general public.

Visit our website at:
http://members.aol.com/USHorus

Ordering Information

Please send me (____) book(s) of Tut-Ankh-Amen
Please send me (____) book(s) of Pyramid Illusions
Please send me (____) book(s) of Historical Deception
to: Name ______________________________
Address ______________________________
City ______________ State ____ Zip ________
Tel. (____) ______________

______ Books @ $9.95 (Tut-Ankh-Amen) = $
______ Books @ $11.95 (Pyramid Illusions) = $
______ Books @ $19.95 (Historical Deception) = $
Add 6% for Pennsylvania residents = $
Add $2.00 shipping & handling for first book = $
for each additional book $1 x ______ = $______
Total = $

Enclose a check/money order payable to:
Bastet Publishing
P.O. Box 7234
Erie, PA 16510, U.S.A.